Finding the Courage to Retire

SIMPLE SOLUTIONS IN A COMPLEX WORLD

Bruce Porter
with Rick Dean

The Resource Center
SPRINGFIELD, MISSOURI

Bruce Porter
The Resource Center
1304 E. Kingsley Street
Springfield, MO 65804
www.resourcecenterinc.com

Book Layout ©2013 BookDesignTemplates.com

Finding the Courage to Retire/Bruce Porter. —1st ed.

ISBN 9781728919003

Contents

Foreword

By **Will Worsham**

Dreams and courage. These are the themes that most struck me as I read Bruce Porter's first book.

For many Americans today, retirement can seem like a dream, and for too many, it seems like a dream that may never happen. Pairing the themes of dreams and courage is nothing new. However, considering them together in the light of retirement is novel. This is because courage is required for dreams to come true — especially the dream of retirement.

Courage, true courage, is birthed from knowledge. To retire without knowledge is not courageous, but foolhardy.

Having worked with Bruce for the past several years in helping people acquire the knowledge necessary to find the courage to retire, I'm pleased to find that kind of information distilled and passed on in this book. As Bruce notes elsewhere in the following chapters, though this book cannot replace the personal guidance of experienced professionals, it hopefully will provide you much of the knowledge and courage necessary to realize the dream of the retirement you've always wanted.

Will Worsham
Managing Attorney, Worsham Law Firm LLC
Springfield, Missouri
June 2018

Will Worsham is not a client of The Resource Center nor was he remunerated for his contributions to this book.

Preface: The Man Who Shaped My Life

He was, quite simply, the most inspirational man I've ever known. Had I not had the honor and privilege of spending my developing years in his presence, I most likely would never have founded The Resource Center, my Springfield, Missouri-based financial services and insurance company. There would be no book you are reading now.

Neil Porter, my beloved father, showed me how to achieve and appreciate prosperity, as well as how to overcome great adversity. He taught me the value of moderation when times are good and the importance of perseverance when times are hard. He instilled in me the power of positive thinking. One of the guiding principles of his life — "Today was a good day, and tomorrow will be even better" — is a precept I continue to live by today.

Dad was an Air Force veteran who began a career in the insurance industry in the early 1960s in Lebanon, Missouri. By his early 30s, he was a top producer for a nationally prominent company (Farmers Insurance Group), and eventually became part of its management team in training and supervising 37 county agents throughout Southwest Missouri.

I was just a boy then, too young to realize how good we had it with Dad pulling down what I now know was a six-figure annual income. Family finances mean relatively little to a seventh-grader. Until, that is, the time when matters beyond Dad's control took it all away.

Dad had his first massive heart attack in 1975 at age 38, way too young. He survived that first fearful night only because of an unauthorized procedure administered by a doctor I am proud to have had as a client for several years. His stressful days as a regional manager were over, and four heart bypasses later he was involuntarily retired and living with the help of Social Security disability payments.

Looking back on that time now, I can't imagine how my father handled the almost overnight disappearance of his ability to earn monthly income. How tough it must have been for him to say, "I can no longer do physical work. Now I have to rely on my mind."

But being suddenly knocked out of the workaday world did not mean my father stopped working to provide for his family.

Even though the very comfortable income we once knew was gone, we never missed a meal. Sure, we had to make adjustments — a lot of them. We were forced to sell off our homestead, which had been in the family for four generations. Dad instead purchased a 40-acre spread upon which we wintered some 390 head of cattle before we could sell them and effectively end our farming and cattle operations.

That's when Dad became involved in real estate, buying and selling small properties at first to generate rental income. In time, I helped manage the rental properties that continued to increase in number until we eventually had more than 180 properties.

Yet, there were some tough financial times in my teen years. Even in the worst of those times, my father remained our provider, our rock. He simply refused to be overwhelmed by the cardiac problems that threatened his life and required a seemingly endless series of heart procedures. He somehow always found a way to persevere. I will always admire him for that.

Looking back on those days some 40 years later, I remember how we got through the worst times. When times are hard, my father would say, you have to work that much harder, do the jobs no one else is willing to do. And, he noted again and again, always do your best to maintain a positive outlook.

I was 19 when I got my license to sell real estate, and 28 when I began selling insurance. Going from a landlord role to the insurance business was like jumping from the frying pan into the fire, and I struggled early on with the rejection you come to know when making cold calls. Nobody was buying anything. I became depressed as I worried about paying my bills with a wife and new baby at home. I was working long hours and eating a lot of peanut butter and jelly sandwiches — when I could afford the jelly, that is.

And yet, I managed to persevere and eventually prosper, largely because I'd watched my Dad do it.

I did it because he was there for me when I was going through my own time of adversity. Even in the worst of those early days as an insurance salesman, when I was sitting alone in the office feeling sorry for myself after an unproductive 12-hour day, I remember my father, my rock, insisting things would eventually get better if I just kept working hard. Always make one more call, he would say. Always try to end each day on a positive note, even if it means working 16 hours until you get that positive result.

These were things Dad would tell his county agents in his management years. They were the principles he employed to get through each day of his own life, the only way he survived 47 different heart treatments and still kept our family from wanting for anything. He showed me, even more than he told me, that you deal with adversity by continuing to move forward, never quitting, always adapting and overcoming adversity. Only when you realize it is possible to get across the swollen creek, he used to say, is when you start to understand that things really can be better.

He had another saying I loved, something he probably took from some cowboy movie. "Son," he would say, "sometimes you've just got to sit back in the saddle, take a big ol' chew and keep riding."

Simple solutions in a complex world

Now, that may seem like an overly simplified approach to life, and I can almost hear you saying how few things in life are ever that simple. That may well be.

But, it's equally true that many times we make things a whole lot more difficult than they have to be. So, when I started my own company in 2001, I adopted a philosophy that became my company motto: "Simple solutions in a complex world."

Not that there was anything simple about the company I envisioned.

My basic goal was to help people plan financially for their futures, help them manage their money. But I also wanted to build a "one-stop shop" that offered every kind of insurance product people might want. I wanted to offer not only life and auto and home insurance, but also health insurance, long-term care insurance, Medicare supplemental insurance and annuities. In addition to offering financial and retirement planning as well as wealth management, I also wanted to offer real estate consulting and estate and tax planning strategies.

I gained experience in all those areas during my previous 10 years of managing insurance services for a major national company. But now I wanted to do things my way instead of having a corporate manager tell me how the company wanted it done.

In building my own completely independent company, I had to develop my own network of people who could help me do all the things I wanted to do. I quickly found, for instance, that I didn't want anything to do with health insurance, but I had a buddy who did nothing but and I would refer people to him. The network concept worked well, and things evolved from there.

That company has grown considerably in the 17 years between its founding and the completion of this book in 2018.

The Resource Center today not only offers the insurance options and financial/retirement planning services described above but now also provides clients with banking and financing options available through my ownership interest in a Springfield bank. We have our own in-house Medicare professional. We've even developed our own home repair/handyman service. We can now accurately say that if we can't find a solution to a financial stumbling block in your life, we can get you access to someone who can.

But even with all this growth in the scope of our business, we still observe the same motto we had from the outset. That is, "Simple solutions in a complex world."

Let's explain that.

Blessed now with the benefit of hindsight, I see how my Dad — in trying to provide for his family after his first heart attack — lost a good deal of whatever wealth he had trying to make the most of money he accumulated as a well-paid regional insurance supervisor. He'd taken some calculated risks with various investment vehicles in the hope of reaping a greater reward. This high risk/high reward concept is, of course, a basic tenet of investing.

The trouble was, he was taking chances with money he couldn't afford to lose. Worse yet, I quickly saw that some of the investment vehicles sold during the go-go days of the 1990s, whose account values had fallen well below Dad's invested principal, were products my national insurance company was pushing me to promote.

How could I offer such products to a client, I asked myself, when I wouldn't sell them to my parents?

In starting my own company, I told myself then, I would work primarily with investment products that provide protection from loss of principal due to market fluctuations. These products also would provide income as well as the potential for growth. Such products understandably reside on the conservative side of the financial spectrum, which is where I choose to live. I've never believed in get-rich-quick concepts; consistent and steady growth is more my style. If you're looking to double an investment in a short window of time, I'm probably not the advisor for you.

Consequently, you will soon find me talking extensively in upcoming chapters about conservative financial vehicles such as the fixed index annuity, an insurance contract that offers contractually assured income as well as protection against loss of principal due to market fluctuations, and which has interest-crediting potential via index tracking.

A note here to readers at the beginning of this book: You will in the following chapters see numerous references to financial products that "protect against loss of principal due to market fluctuations." These are words used often in the financial services industry, mostly for legal reasons. They are not always words commonly used by people who visit my office or engage me in casual conversations. Most of these people, especially those nearing or in retirement, express their goals and objectives in terms of finding financial tools that bring "safety and security" to their retirement nest eggs. They talk of also wanting some "growth" in their retirement accounts. These use a common language with well-understood meanings, but this is language that professionals in the financial service industry avoid, for a variety of reasons. Because no one financial product can provide absolute, 100 percent safety or security from every risk, these terms should not be used by financial professionals to describe them, and rightly so.

Even so, I believe strongly in the same things many of my clients are seeking. Their often-expressed desire for "safety and security" and "growth and income" in retirement are cornerstones of my philosophy. I hear what they are saying, and though I must often respond with guarded terms, I want my readers to know from the outset that I understand what they are seeking.

To be sure, conservative financial vehicles such as the fixed index annuity ("FIA") are not the type of sexy investment you might have pursued during your working years, those days when you had ample time hopefully to recover any loss a higher-risk investment might incur. Moreover, when you were still working and bringing in a steady income, you likely didn't worry as much about the effect a market decline would have on your future retirement income.

But people either approaching or in retirement — and we'll spend much of this book talking about retirement planning, a large part of the company business I handle — are understandably slow to embrace investments with a high level of volatility. I'm talking here about investments whose performance bounces up and down with each change of direction in the stock market. These are investments that offer no assurance against loss and no guarantee of future income.

In my nearly three decades in the financial services industry, I've seen too many people taking too many gambles in the hopes of getting a couple additional points in the return on their investments.

There is a time and place for doing that, of course, but that time is not in the years approaching retirement. When the time of one's life shifts from the asset accumulation phase of our working years to the distribution/income phase of retirement, I see no sense in taking unnecessary risks with an entire portfolio in the hope of realizing a 6 to 8 percent gain when it is possible to allocate a portion of the retirement assets to insurance-backed products that provide the opportunity for competitive interest credits along with contractual guarantees.

Now, it should go without saying that clients with a greater tolerance for risk are free to consider financial products that offer the potential for greater returns on investment. Of course, we offer such products at The Resource Center.

Still, even a conservatively managed portfolio carries no guarantee against loss of principal due to market fluctuation. For many of my clients approaching or in retirement who say they have little or no tolerance for market-related risk — and frankly, most of the people I see fall into this category — even a small element of risk is more than they are willing to take. Many consequently seek products whose income-paying ability is backed by insurance companies, which offer protection against loss of principal due to market volatility. It is important that a client understand the workings of any financial tool they are considering and the purposes for which it was intended.

This emphasis on protecting your life's saving from loss of principal is something I advocated initially from watching my father's financial struggles. It became amplified later in my career when watching clients hit the panic button upon seeing their stock portfolio in free falls during the dot-com bubble burst of 1999, and especially during the Great Recession of late 2007 through early 2009.

To be sure, the market bounced back nicely from those dark days. Yet, my concerns were reinforced again recently when — during an overall market rally — a prominent Springfield auto parts manufacturer whose stock is a component of many of my clients' 401(k)s slowly lost $100 a share in just a year's time.

This is why I believe in using financial products that provide protection against loss of principal due to market fluctuations as the foundation of a pre-retirement/retirement portfolio. These insurance products provide contractually guaranteed income, those regularly scheduled annuity payments guaranteed by the claims-paying ability of an insurance company to last as long as you do. It's why I believe in insurance products such as the fixed index annuity that protects principal against losses due to market fluctuation while offering the potential for conservative interest crediting through tracking of an index with no actual participation in that index or an underlying stock market.

Some people may be skeptical about the simplicity of this product. But if your objectives are protection from losses due to market volatility, as well as income and growth, insurance-based products such as fixed index annuities and fixed indexed universal life insurance are products that can accomplish exactly that. Again, simple solutions in a complex world.

This is the kind of customer-oriented service mentality I believe would have made my father proud.

Neil Porter, who once didn't think he'd live to see age 40, passed away in 2015 at age 78 after surviving more than 40 heart procedures. His approach to dealing with life's ups and downs will remain with me long after his passing.

Now, it's my turn to give something back. It's why I'm writing this book.

In it, I hope to help readers deal with the many "what if" scenarios that can make retirement a scary prospect to some people. What if I run out of money in retirement? What if I need long-term health care? What if I don't know nearly enough about Social Security or Medicare?

Throughout this book, we will discuss preparations you can make now — in the years prior to retirement — that can help address much of the uncertainty people have about life in the post-workaday world. For it is only when one acquires the knowledge necessary to travel the unknown road ahead — when one truly understands that it's possible to cross the swollen creek, as my Dad once said — that we find the courage to retire.

CHAPTER 1

Plan to Make Your Dreams Come True

E veryone is entitled to their dreams, especially when it comes to retirement.

After 30 to 40 or more years in the daily grind of the workaday world — a time when we may have achieved some of our dreams while seeing others go unfulfilled — we entertain new visions of life in retirement. We look forward to having more time to do the things we could do only sparingly in our working years. We dream of doing more hunting, fishing, golfing. We dream of spending more time with our kids and grandkids. We dream of travel to distant places we've never seen or treating ourselves to a "luxury" we once thought unattainable. To owning that vacation home in Florida or Arizona perhaps, or taking a trip to Europe or a series of ocean cruises. Suddenly it all begins to seem like something other than a fantasy.

There's nothing wrong with having big dreams, especially if you're willing to do the work and planning necessary to turn them into reality.

Sadly, though, some people don't do nearly enough real planning in the years prior to retirement to make their dreams come true.

Don't misunderstand; many folks make investments on their future throughout their working years. They've paid into Social Security for decades. They likely put a small part of each regular paycheck into a company-sponsored 401(k) retirement plan. They may have purchased some life insurance along the way. They might even have opened some brokerage-account investments — maybe as part of an individual retirement account (IRA) — with stocks, bonds, mutual funds, exchange-traded funds (ETFs) or an annuity or two. As someone who advises clients on retirement planning, I will always appreciate people who invest whatever they can when they can with an eye on a time when they no longer *have* to work.

At the same time, however, I also know investing by itself is not always enough to secure the lifestyle we dream of having in retirement. Here's why.

When estimating retirement income, most people know they will receive a fixed monthly payment from Social Security. A fortunate few might also receive income from a traditional company pension, though these have become a disappearing breed since the early part of the 21st century. Many people will supplement their Social Security income with a monthly payment from their 401(k) or IRA.

Others will take additional income from at-risk market investments — that is, investments whose values rise and fall with the daily ebbs and flows of the stock or bond markets. These investors have likely been advised that they can take an annual income of around 4 percent from such investments and still have income-producing assets for 25 to 30 years of retirement. This is the famous "4 percent rule," a conventional-wisdom staple of the financial services industry.

Well, the 4 percent rule didn't provide much comfort for people who depended on retirement income from at-risk assets — whether in a 401(k), IRA or brokerage account — whose value took a major plummet during the dot-com bubble burst of 1999 and 2000. A few years later, this "rule" was all but shredded during the Great Recession of 2007 to 2009 when many market-risk assets lost 40 to 50 percent of their value and produced a corresponding free fall in many — if not most — retirement accounts.

Suddenly, retirees who had been taking 4 percent from pre-recession accounts of, say, $250,000 — $10,000 in annual income — now found themselves receiving only $6,000 when taking the same 4 percent from those same accounts whose value had diminished in just two years to only $150,000. Moreover, they quickly saw that continuing to take 4 percent a year in such market conditions would wipe out their retirement savings in considerably less time than they'd been led to expect.

When reality hits hard

Granted, the overall health of the stock market came back slowly and steadily in the years following the Great Recession. In time, many of the retirement nest eggs that took a devastating hit in the first decade of the current century recovered their value and grew during the following decade.

Not that this was necessarily a significant comfort to many retirees in 2008 who, lacking the ability to foresee the future, sweated out major concerns about running out of money. Such concerns raised their head yet again here in Southwest Missouri in 2017 when a prominent regional employer saw its stock price fall more than 40 percent a share in a very short period of time. This decline happened not because of anything this otherwise solid company did, but because of negative sector-wide comments made by a famous national investor.

You think retirement dreams don't get a sudden wake-up call during such times, however temporary they might be?

Retirees who are able to avoid total panic — and not everyone can do this — tell themselves with a reasonable degree of confidence that market conditions will get better over time and that their retirement savings accounts will improve accordingly. But even these people know they no longer have the time they once did to wait for the rebound.

We consequently adjust our dreams or change our lifestyles to reflect a suddenly tightened budget. If we're lucky, such adjustments are minor. Maybe we dine out less often than we did when the cash flow was better. Maybe we make fewer out-of-town trips. Maybe we don't go to as many Cardinals or Chiefs games as we once dreamed of doing.

Maybe we even go back to work, either on a full- or part-time basis, whether we want to or not.

Making adjustments during times of adversity is a normal part of life. I personally watched my father and my family make them after his first heart attack affected his income-creating ability as a relatively young man.

Expect the unexpected

In the time since those teenage years, however, I've also come to appreciate how a more conservative approach to saving and investing — especially in the years leading up to retirement — can help people in retirement better deal with the frequent market volatility and crazy economic swings that can steal our sleep and threaten our dreams.

To repeat a point made previously, the years leading up to and entering retirement represent a new phase of one's life. It's a transition period from the accumulation phase of your working years to the preservation and distribution phase of your retirement years. In short, you are turning assets you amassed as a working person into income that will serve you for the remainder of your life when you're no longer working.

Making this conversion often requires basic changes in one's approach to money, an approach that puts a premium on creating a foundation of protection from losses due to market fluctuations. If I might be allowed to use a baseball analogy, it is perfectly fine to swing for the fences as a younger saver/investor. Retirement, however, is a time to accept walks and singles to the opposite field.

As I mentioned previously, one of the many topics we'll be discussing in upcoming chapters is developing streams of reliable, contractually guaranteed, sustained income that survive as long as we do in retirement. Such income typically does not come from the "home run" returns of high-risk/high-reward investments. But slow-and-steady — advancing one base at a time, to return to my baseball analogy — works perfectly well in retirement.

This is income that is contractually required to be paid directly into your bank account on a regular schedule. Once called "mailbox income," it comes from Social Security and defined-benefit pensions as well as annuities. This is income that is not affected by the ever-changing winds of the stock market. This is income produced by financial products that protect against loss of your invested principal due to market fluctuations. This is income you can count on receiving for life, income that helps establish an essential financial foundation of your retirement plan and gives you the option to expose at least some part of your retirement savings — whatever level of risk you are comfortable in taking — to at-risk investments with the potential for growth.

Developing these sustainable lifetime income streams as part of a comprehensive retirement income plan — something that involves much more than merely saying one "should" be able to take 4 percent from retirement assets annually and not outlive one's money — helps a retiree better prepare for the unexpected.

Such a plan should tell you exactly where your income is coming from, how much you can spend annually, and how much you should have remaining at various levels of retirement. Such a plan also should consider options — available in many of today's annuities and life insurance policies — that allow for proceeds to be used to help cover at least some of the expenses associated with long-term medical or nursing care, if certain conditions are met. Such a plan should also include provisions for income for surviving spouses and loved ones.

It is my belief that only when a person or couple has such a plan in place prior to retirement that one can truly begin the process of turning their retirement dreams into reality.

To be sure, financial adjustments are sometimes necessary even after establishing a foundation of reliable, sustainable income. Life throws us curves, and no one can promise that our dreams will come true.

With a solid financial base in place, however, adjustments become just that. We rent a Florida timeshare rather than buy a condo. We buy a used bass boat instead of a new one. We visit the Tetons instead of the Alps. We tour Tucson instead of Tuscany.

Bottom line, your retirement dreams don't have to vanish, or become a nightmare, due to world events beyond your control.

CHAPTER 2

Finding the Courage to Retire

I didn't really need a dictionary to tell me about the inverse relationship between fear and courage, but sometimes it's nice to have official confirmation.

The Merriam-Webster dictionary, for example, defines the word "courage" as "Mental or moral strength to venture, persevere and withstand danger, fear or difficulty." The internet website dictionary.com defines "courage" even more simply as "The quality of mind or spirit that enables a person to face difficulty, danger, pain, etc., without fear."

Having concerns, apprehensions and fear of the unknown are all part of preparing for retirement. The process of overcoming such fears led me to call this book, "Finding the Courage to Retire."

Making the transition from the working world one has known for 30 to 40 years into a new world of retirement raises understandable concerns, if not outright fear, on the part of many people preparing to take this big step. If there is one central point I hope to impart in this book, it's that taking this leap into the unknown requires a certain level of courage. Finding that courage comes in large part from working through all the "what-if" questions that inevitably precede retirement. Sadly, a lot of people don't do that.

What are the most significant fears people must overcome to find the courage to retire?

The most common one I hear from clients is the fear that an individual or couple will live longer than the money they've saved for retirement. The "Will I run out of money in retirement?" fear is a huge one, but it only scratches the surface.

Among other commonly expressed concerns:

• The fear of financial and physical devastation if faced with a long-term health condition, especially one that requires assisted living or nursing care. The fear of becoming a burden on loved ones, or of simply being "put away" and forgotten, goes hand-in-hand.

• The fear that Social Security — a principal source of retirement income for many Americans — may not be there when we need it. With that comes concerns that people don't know nearly as much as they should about how to go about receiving this source of income designed to help support them for the remainder of their lives.

• The fear of becoming unproductive, of losing one's sense of worth, of living out our days without a purpose. "What will I do with all this spare time in retirement?" is a great unknown for many people, even those with long-standing dreams.

Again, these are fears of an uncertain future, worries about an impending lifestyle change that is vastly different from anything we experienced during our working years. Yet, these are very real worries that affect people from a psychological standpoint, and they must be addressed at some point before we become truly comfortable with the idea of retirement.

That's why I say it takes courage to pull the trigger on your decision to retire.

Overcoming fears of the unknown

Education is the key to addressing these "what-if" questions. An old adage suggests knowledge is power — in this case, the power to know we can acquire a large degree of control over our retirement future.

Admittedly, no one ever has *complete* control over their future. But when people acquire a better understanding of the important issues they face in retirement, they gain confidence. They prepare knowing decisions they make regarding their retirement future will at least be calculated decisions. Finding the courage to retire involves planning and learning and acquiring the knowledge necessary to overcome any uncertainty.

You learn, as my father liked to say, that you *can* cross the swollen creek.

This courage ultimately comes when you learn more about how things work in retirement. When you learn exactly how your income will be produced, and from which sources it will come. When you know which portions of your savings will produce income for the rest of your life and which parts you might expose to market risks in the hope of seeing greater growth. When you understand what you can afford to do in retirement, as well as what you can't. When you become more comfortable with the prospect that, should an emergency arise — a long-term health crisis, perhaps — you have financial resources available to see you through, as well as people you can count on to say, "Hey, I've got your back."

The courage to retire comes after you understand exactly how Medicare will work and how supplemental insurance will help pay bills that Medicare doesn't cover. It comes after you learn how Social Security works and how your decision on when to first began taking benefits affects the monthly check you will receive for life. It comes after you understand what "provisional income" is and how it affects the taxation of your Social Security benefits. It comes after you know how to provide for a surviving spouse or heirs.

Armed with this advance planning and an understanding of how you will deal with the myriad situations that await you in retirement, you eventually acquire the courage to proceed confidently. This is the point at which you will feel most comfortable about making the leap into retirement.

The trouble, however, is that many people have no idea how to even start this process. Too many simply don't know what they don't know. They don't know who to talk to, or maybe they're afraid of the cost of retirement planning. It's part of the reason many people don't do any financial planning, tax planning or estate planning.

I talk to people all the time who don't know what provisional income is. They have no idea how it can affect the taxation of their Social Security benefits and their overall tax structure — often the second biggest drain (next to health care costs) on the typical retirement nest egg.

They don't understand required minimum distributions (RMDs), those mandatory withdrawals from tax-deferred accounts the IRS requires beginning at age 70½. Being required to withdraw this money from IRAs or 401(k)s — whether you need the money or not — can increase provisional income and potentially increase taxes on Social Security. This becomes a double whammy that can force retirees into a higher tax bracket, something you truly want to avoid in retirement.

Which brings us back to the purpose of this book.

My idea in writing this book stems from a desire to help people — some of them potential clients, perhaps — navigate the unknown waters that await them in retirement. Using some simple solutions — primarily through the establishment of sustainable income that will last the rest of one's life — to better help people handle otherwise complex matters.

Life marches on in retirement. Learning how to handle a new routine, as well as deal with the unexpected curves life throws at all of us, is part of preparing for that new life. Being prepared for something new is when one finally has the confidence to say, "I've had enough; I'm ready to retire."

Let's look with more detail into the process of overcoming some of the specific fears described above.

Will I outlive my money?

I hear this concern voiced most often by clients whose retirement savings are invested primarily in assets exposed to the ever-shifting winds of the stock market.

In my opinion, too many people set up their retirement income plan based on taking a set percentage from market-risk income. Consequently, someone planning to take retirement income of, say, 4 percent a year from a pool of $500,000 in market-risk accounts suddenly starts losing sleep when those accounts lose value — as happened in 2008 during the Great Recession — and they find themselves needing the same level of income from accounts now worth only, say, $300,000.

Now, it goes without saying that a Great Recession — as well as a routine recession, bear market or even a typical market correction — can cause consternation for anyone taking income from market-exposed assets. Nothing I present here will completely eliminate those concerns.

Even so, it's possible to minimize such worries, at least, when much or most of one's retirement nest egg is allocated to assets that produce streams of sustainable income.

I use the term "sustainable income" a lot, so let's define it here. Sustainable income is money you can count on receiving on a monthly, quarterly or annual basis. It is a return on assets you know will be deposited directly into your bank account for as long as you live. It is money that is not dependent primarily on the rise or fall of the stock market. It is money you will never run out of.

Sustainable income is of the utmost importance when making the decision to retire. Sustainable income is more important than growth; it's more important than an account balance. Sustainable income is income that will never run out, and it's something people don't think nearly enough about.

Where does such money come from?

Social Security, with its government-backed promise to pay you a monthly benefit for as long as you live, is the primary source for many people. Annuity payments, which are backed by the claims-paying ability of the insurance companies that write the contracts, are another source. Many insurance policies with "living benefits" — optional riders, usually added for an additional fee, that allow the insured to use the policy's death benefits while still alive should certain conditions be met — may also provide a source of sustainable income.

We'll talk in more detail later in this chapter about Social Security, then later in the book about how income is generated by annuities and life insurance.

For now, however, let's look at how sustainable income can help a person either nearing or in retirement better handle concerns about running out of retirement income.

We're talking here about establishing an income plan, one that supplements income from Social Security and any work-related pension (if you're still lucky enough to have one of those).

This is why I believe as strongly as I do in financial products — especially the fixed index annuity, which I'll discuss in greater detail in a later chapter — that produce lifetime income with no market risk to your invested capital. These are products that provide protection of principal from losses due to market fluctuations as well as income and the potential for growth. These are products that give you the confidence to know you will have a source of income for as long as you live.

Look, you've worked and saved your whole life. Now, you're retired. You don't want to even think about the safety of your money. You want to live comfortably without worrying about market volatility, or about what's going on in North Korea and how that might affect your retirement savings. You dealt with market volatility in your 401(k) throughout your entire working life. Now you're done with that, and you just want income you know will be there.

Taking much (or most) of your retirement income from guaranteed sources can help remove much (or most) of the worry that inevitably arises should the majority of your retirement income be generated from assets exposed to the market.

Keep in mind that it's perfectly fine, and even desirable, to have at least some retirement money exposed to conservative or moderate market risk in the hope of gaining at least a moderate reward if your personal risk tolerance allows for it.

Based on my experience, however, you will feel more comfortable doing so when you have a solid base of sustainable income to support any possible weakening in the market. Such a foundation of sustainable income often helps retired people resist the urge to make ill-timed sell decisions during market corrections, as we'll illustrate in an example.

The rise and fall of XYZ

My prospective client was in a bind shortly before he came to see me.

He was 60 years old and had plans to retire at age 62. Much of his retirement savings were invested in XYZ stock, a fictional name for the real company at which he worked. XYZ had been doing very well in the years when he was purchasing shares in the $220 to $285 range as part of his 401(k).

And then one day, a nationally prominent investor made some negative comments about the manufacturing industry in which XYZ operated. Within a short period of time, the company's stock price fell more than $100 a share from its 52-week high.

The man panicked; he admits it. His 401(k) account value had fallen more than $100,000 in just over a week. Not knowing how far the price plunge would go, he sold almost all his XYZ shares at a $175 price, which eventually proved to be the bottom of the fall. He felt beaten, and now he wondered if he could afford to retire at age 65, three years later than he originally planned.

I wish I'd known him earlier. Not because I had a crystal ball when it came to XYZ; I didn't. Rather, we might have done some things in advance of the plunge that might have helped him better deal with the fall.

Hindsight is always 20:20. But in looking back, I can't help but wish the gentleman had done an in-service rollover of at least a large part of his 401(k) savings into something more conservative — perhaps an indexed annuity as part of a personal IRA. With the bulk of his money now protected from losses due to market volatility while still having the potential for growth — and guaranteeing regular income payments for the rest of his life — he would have been in better position to ride out the downturn in XYZ's stock, a company both he and I still like very much.

Knowing he had a base of principally protected, sustainable annuity income in place — meaning he didn't have to depend totally on income from a stock declining in value — he might have retained more of his XYZ shares while waiting for the gradual rebound he believed was coming. XYZ's stock price eventually did just that — it was back in the $275 range within six months after hitting its low — and its recovery would have given him several options.

He would not have to be overly aggressive to get back much of what he lost in the mere two years before his desired retirement date. That, in fact, might have been the worst thing he could have done. As a general rule, given his age of 60, there is no way I would advise him to put more than 40 percent of his retirement savings in investments exposed to market volatility. Obviously, everyone's situation is unique, and the allocation of their money will be tailored to address this, but 40 percent is my general rule of thumb to be used as a starting point.

With an established foundation of sustainable income, however, he could afford to be more cautious. As the stock price slowly recovered, he would be in a position to gradually take chips off the table. He might, for example, move 5 points from every 10 points of recovery into something more conservative, perhaps as additional contributions to his annuity or a conservatively managed mutual fund. In time, he might well find XYZ's stock price at a level where he would be more comfortable taking income through periodic sales of his shares.

The point here is, having an adequate portion of your retirement assets — those that will serve as the foundation of your day-to-day income — allocated to financial products that generate sustainable income has the potential to put you in a better position to avoid making panicked, knee-jerk decisions when volatility affects market-exposed assets. Riding out a downturn can be difficult for anyone. But knowing your retirement savings aren't totally exposed to the changing market winds can help you better weather the occasional storm.

How will I handle a long-term health crisis?

Let's be honest about something right here at the start of this discussion. No amount of advance planning in the world will enable a person or their loved ones to completely escape all of the physical, emotional and financial pain that can come with a debilitating, life-changing injury, illness or disease.

Having said that, let's also note that developing at least some kind of plan for dealing financially with long-term health care is better than having no plan at all. Yet sadly, far too many people have no plan at all.

There are any number of ways to build a contingency plan that provides at least some financial protection from the potentially devastating costs of long-term care in retirement.

• You can buy a long-term care insurance policy. While this makes sense for some, be aware that this can be costly both in the initial purchase price and if premiums increase as you get older. Moreover, if you don't actually use this insurance, you have no return on the premiums you paid.

• You can consider annuity and permanent life insurance policies that include riders (sometimes available for an additional fee) designed to allow access to the policy funds to help with the costs associated with terminal illness or long-term care over a period of time.

• You can make your own contributions to a tax-advantageous health savings account (HSA). Money contributed to such accounts is not subject to federal tax in the year of the contribution, and distributions taken later for qualified medical expenses also are not subject to federal tax or penalty.

Again, having at least some kind of contingency plan can be a comfort. Even in a worst-case situation, one in which you become incapacitated and are not completely aware of everything going on around you, there can be comfort in knowing in advance that your loved ones have some financial protection.

Allow me to illustrate the above point with a true-life story.

Restoring calm amid a health crisis storm

My client was 65 at the time. He'd just sold a successful business for several million dollars and was looking forward to a new phase of his life.

He looked to be in great shape to do so. He seemed in good health when he and his wife purchased a vacation home in Missouri, along with a boat and two new cars. He had various retirement savings accounts that were growing nicely and from which he planned to start taking income at age 70. His kids were grown and living their own productive lives.

And then one day my client was cut down by a stroke.

I got the call late that afternoon. The emergency room nurse told me my client was asking that I come to the hospital, which I did as quickly as possible. He was in stable condition, but the effects of the stroke were obvious as he spoke. He clearly was panicked and worried, and his first fear seemed to be the prospect of paying for all the rehabilitation and extended care he would need during his recovery.

We talked initially about the many things he had done well in preparing for this kind of health crisis. We talked about how his recently purchased Medicare Supplemental insurance with Part F coverage would cover 100 percent of his hospital and physician expenses, as well as providing up to 100 days of treatment in a rehab center.

We looked at a printout projecting his long-term financial situation. He saw he had both cash in hand (through the recent sale of his business) and cash in reserve through long-held investments. He also was reminded that an estate plan was in place.

He soon seemed to realize, because of the advance planning he had done, he had the resources to stop worrying about money and instead begin concentrating on his all-important recovery process.

A year later he was doing well on the road to recovery. His work in home rehab helped him become certified to drive again. He and his wife sold one of their homes to downsize, which also helped them avoid tapping into their retirement reserves.

My client deserves all the credit for putting himself and his family in a position to better weather the storm of his life-changing stroke. He'd worked hard all his life, earned well, saved well, planned effectively. He already had done many of the essential elements of retirement planning: developed sources of sustainable income, made provisions for long-term health care, understood the importance of Medicare supplemental insurance, developed an estate plan.

My client's prognosis for full recovery remains to be seen, but, from a financial standpoint, his early preparations put him in a position to be hopeful.

Can I depend on Social Security?

Allow me to answer the above question in three words. Yes. And no.

The "yes" answer means I believe Social Security will be with us for many years to come — for the lifetime, I expect, of anyone reading this book.

Sure, there are credible forecasts predicting that the Social Security Trust Fund — the account into which almost all workers contribute through payroll taxes — will have a negative balance beginning sometime around 2034.[1] Even so, I still believe that this popular, long-standing social safety net will be preserved for generations to come. If ever something was "too big to fail" — for

[1] Donna Borak. CNN Money. "Social Security trust fund projected to tap out in 17 years." July 13, 2017.
https://money.cnn.com/2017/07/13/news/economy/social-security-trust-fund-projection/index.html

instance, something that provides income for 90 percent of Americans age 65 or older, as well as for disabled workers and survivors — Social Security is it.

That doesn't mean, however, that major changes might not be forthcoming.

The all-important full retirement age (FRA) — the age at which a person is eligible to receive their full Social Security benefit — is likely to increase again. It's already risen from age 65 to 66 (for people born from 1943 through 1954) and is on a gradual upward climb to age 67 for people born after 1960. (See the "full retirement age" chart in the following chapter.) I wouldn't be surprised to see FRA extended to age 70 sometime before 2034.

I also can foresee other possible changes as well, such as reducing cost-of-living adjustments or payments to people receiving disability benefits. I also would not be surprised to see the current 15.3 percent payroll withholding tax — which funds Social Security and Medicare and is evenly divided between employees and employers — increased in future years.

But back to the above question: Can I depend on Social Security? Well, if the question is asked in the context of, "Can I depend on Social Security to fund my retirement?" then my answer has to be "no."

I say "no" mainly because times have changed considerably since Social Security was established in 1935 as part of the recovery from the Great Depression. Part of the idea then was to establish an economic safety net for older workers so they could retire at age 65 and open up jobs for younger people desperately needing work. Social Security would provide basic retirement income, but even President Franklin Roosevelt understood the new program had its limits.

"This law represents a cornerstone in a structure that is being built, but is by no means complete," FDR said at the Aug. 14, 1935, signing of the Social Security Bill.

As the recovery from the Depression continued through the late 1930s and into the years of World War II and beyond, more companies began adding company-sponsored pensions as an incentive to retain productive workers. These defined-benefit pensions, when coupled with Social Security, allowed several generations of American workers to expect a reasonably comfortable lifestyle in retirement.

Today, however, those company pension programs are largely a thing of the past. Social Security consequently provides 90 percent or more of all retirement income for 23 percent of older married beneficiaries, and about 43 percent for unmarried ones.[2] Without additional sources of retirement income, many of those people struggle to get by on a monthly benefit that in 2017 averaged only $1,369 for retired workers, according to figures from the Social Security Administration.

It only makes sense, then, that if Social Security is at least a primary source of retirement income — as it is for 50 percent of married couples and 71 percent of unmarried people who receive at least half of their retirement income from the program — a beneficiary should try to receive the optimum benefit for which they are eligible.

Receiving that optimum benefit requires at least a basic understanding of the rules of Social Security. The program is important enough that I will devote the entire next chapter to its essential workings.

What am I going to do with all that free time? Or, the fear of being useless

Allow me to ask a rhetorical question that has no correct response.

Who's the grouchiest person you know?

---

[2] Social Security Administration, ssa.gov. "Social Security Fact Sheet." 2017.

It could be anyone at any age, certainly. In my experience, though, it's often the retired guy who sits on his front porch griping about the speeders on his street or the kids and dogs on his lawn. My experience also tells me that if you ever get such a person to talk honestly about why they are so unhappy, they'll express some variation of being bored, of not knowing what to do with all their time, about feeling unneeded.

The fear of becoming that kind of person — or of sharing some of the problems that lead to such a cranky disposition — concerns some people as they approach retirement. What will I do with all this new-found free time? What do I do when there is nothing I absolutely *have* to do?

The fear of suddenly becoming unnecessary is very real for people, especially for those with a strong sense of self-worth. To be sure, people who for years had to supervise others might welcome the chance to shed that responsibility, but it's equally true that others will miss it. The sense of becoming "not needed" in retirement is very vivid for many active people.

Not that anyone ever plans to be inactive heading into retirement.

As we discussed in the previous chapter, everyone has dreams of how their retirement will be spent. We look forward to taking more or longer vacations, spending more time with the kids and grandkids, playing more golf or tennis or going hunting or fishing with friends. Lifelong hobbies will now get more of our attention.

Then, over time, we often find those plans changing, sometimes through no fault of our own.

Maybe you find that retirement is costlier than you estimated, and you don't have the resources to do all the traveling you wanted. Maybe you discover that now that you have additional time to spend with adult children and their children, they now are too busy to spend additional time with you. ("Say, Mom, when did you say you were heading home?") Your friends who talked for years about all the rounds of golf you'll play together in retirement, or all the extended fishing or hunting trips you'll take, suddenly find their own reasons for cutting back on those big plans. Your hobby begins to lose its appeal as it becomes more of a full-time endeavor. Boredom becomes a too-frequent companion.

You gradually may find yourself becoming more isolated, especially as good friends and loved ones leave us or become physically or mentally disabled. Loneliness can settle in; depression isn't far behind. Our daily aches and pains seem more pronounced, and the natural deterioration of the body seems to be happening faster. Such is the cycle of life.

How folks deal with these changes is entirely up to them, but I have some advice I'm not hesitant to offer to clients who raise the subject.

In a nutshell, make plans to make yourself useful, to stay active and productive.

Take on a part-time job, engage in volunteer work, make yourself available to a nonprofit organization doing good work. Become a consultant or even a mentor to a young person or young worker. Open your mind to things you never thought you would do, such as running for public office (if you've got a thick skin) or getting involved with local-issue campaigns. Consider challenges you once considered unimaginable.

Above all else, do the things you enjoy doing.

Continuing to work in retirement — if working involves something you enjoy doing, that is — has benefits in several areas. Taking a part-time job that you enjoy keeps you active, keeps your mind functioning, keeps you in the game and feeling sharp. It keeps you in contact with people, helps maintain a social life. It can keep you feeling useful, needed, necessary.

You like golf, or just being around golfers? Look for a part-time job at a golf course, a driving range, a sporting goods store, maybe even a putt-putt where you can help kids. You like exercising and being outdoors? Mow grass, walk dogs, volunteer to tend the grounds for the local parks and rec. Want to get around people again because you're a friendly person? Consider working in a department store. They'll pay you a few bucks, maybe even offer some kind of store-related benefit. And if you get tired of working, you can always, you know, retire.

Again, the main idea here is to work for the paycheck you love as opposed to the one you need.

Many people continue to work in retirement because they *have* to, but the goal should be to work only because you *want* to. Here once again is where advance planning and investing and developing streams of sustainable income can make the big difference between *wanting* to work and *having* to work.

Control the things within your control

All of the above issues discussed in this chapter contribute to my observation that it takes courage to retire.

Admittedly, we never have complete control over all the things that come at us in retirement, just as in life. After all, even physically fit people get diseases, and bad things occasionally happen to good people.

Even so, knowing something about the road ahead is essential to making plans that deal with that road's twists, turns and detours. You will never have all the answers — understandable considering that you can't know all the questions. Still, with a basic understanding of the most common concerns facing people heading into retirement — maintaining lifetime income, dealing with long-term health care, handling the psychological strain of remaining useful — a person can at least prepare a foundation upon which to base their retirement dreams.

It's when you build that foundation of sustainable income, as well as resources for long-term care and a plan for both personal and financial growth that a person becomes more comfortable with the idea of leaving the daily working world behind.

It is my belief that at the end of that process is when you find the courage to finally say, "I've had it; I'm done. The money I've saved and invested is protected and growing, and it will be there to take care of my spouse and me. We're as prepared as we can be to handle an emergency, health-related or otherwise. I understand how my income will be produced, and I have a basic understanding of what my expenses (including taxes) will be. I have plans in place to provide for my spouse and heirs when I'm no longer with them.

"I've now found the courage I was looking for. I'm now ready to retire."

CHAPTER 3

The Essentials of Social Security

As we discussed in the previous chapter, because Social Security is a primary source of income for many retired people, it is essential to understand at least its basic rules — as well as a few of its bells and whistles — in order to receive the maximum benefit for which you are entitled.

Let's first take a minute to discuss that word "entitled."

Yes, Social Security is often referred to as a "government entitlement," usually by politicians who should probably substitute the word "obligation" for "entitlement." That's because Social Security recipients are "entitled" only in the sense that they (along with their employers) have spent years investing money into the program and subsequently are "entitled" to see some, all, or more than all that investment returned to them in retirement.

Entire books have been written about a program that has over 500 rules and regulations, but let's take a chapter here to highlight the essentials. Note in advance that we'll be talking exclusively here about retirement options as opposed to the disability and survivor elements of the program.

How does one qualify for Social Security?

A worker earns a full Social Security benefit by amassing 40 "work credits" over the course of a working career. A credit is earned with every $1,320 in income (according to 2018 requirements), meaning a person earning $5,280 annually can earn a maximum of four work credits a year. A 10-year work history — which does not mean 10 *consecutive* years of work — will qualify a person for a full Social Security benefit.

How much your "full benefit" will be depends on how much you paid in payroll taxes — also known as FICA withholding — during your working years.

Ever since 1990, American workers have paid 6.25 percent of every paycheck into the Old Age, Survivors and Disability Insurance program (OASDI), and another 1.45 percent for Medicare health insurance. That 7.65 percent total is matched by the worker's employer for a total contribution of 15.3 percent. A self-employed person pays the full 15.3 percent as both an employee and an employer.

Needless to say, the more you earned, the more you paid in withholding and the bigger your benefit will be when it comes time to collect Social Security benefits. Note: There is a maximum amount of benefit that can be paid each month — $2,788 in 2018 — as well as a lid on the amount of annual income ($127,200) subject to payroll taxes. A person approaching the time to consider taking Social Security can get a very accurate estimate of what his or her benefit will be by establishing an online account at www.ssa.gov/myaccount.

When to begin receiving Social Security

You are eligible to receive your full benefit upon reaching full retirement age (see chart), but you do not have to wait until FRA to begin taking Social Security. A qualified person can begin taking benefits as early as age 62, but benefits taken "early" will be permanently reduced — emphasis on the word "permanently" — by the amount of time between the start of benefits and the recipient's FRA.

Your Full Retirement Age

Year of Birth	Full Retirement Age
1937 or earlier	65
1938	65 and 2 months
1939	65 and 4 months
1940	65 and 6 months
1941	65 and 8 months
1942	65 and 10 months
1943—1954	66
1955	66 and 2 months
1956	66 and 4 months
1957	66 and 6 months
1958	66 and 8 months
1959	66 and 10 months
1960 or later	67

Social Security Administration. 2017. "Full Retirement Age."
https://www.ssa.gov/planners/retire/retirechart.html.

That permanent reduction is approximately 6.25 percent each year. Thus, a person with an FRA of 66 who begins taking benefits four years early at age 62 will see his/her monthly benefit reduced by 25 percent. In numbers, a full monthly benefit of $2,000 at FRA will be permanently reduced (not counting annual cost-of-living adjustments) by 25 percent to $1,500 if taken at age 62. A person with an FRA of 67 who begins taking benefits five years early at 62 will see his/her projected monthly benefit reduced some 30 percent. That person's projected full benefit of $2,000 at FRA would fall to $1,400 if taken at age 62.

The explanation for the reduced benefit is obvious. In taking benefits early, you will, in theory, receive more monthly payments over your lifetime than will a person who waits until FRA. Those payments must necessarily be reduced.

Now for some upbeat news.

A person who delays taking benefits for several years after reaching FRA can receive a permanently *increased* benefit. Through the receipt of delayed retirement credits, a person's monthly benefit will increase 8 percent every year between FRA and age 70, the point at which delayed retirement credits end.

In numbers, our above person with the $2,000 projected monthly benefit at an FRA of 66 will see that benefit increase 32 percent (8 percent a year times 4 years) to $2,640 if waiting until age 70 to take benefits. A person projected to receive a $2,000 benefit at an FRA of 67 will see that benefit rise 24 percent to $2,480 three years later at age 70.

Clearly, waiting until FRA or later means larger monthly payments to people who don't pull the Social Security trigger at the first opportunity. In theory, however, those patient folks will receive a lower number of payments over the typical American life expectancy.

But what about people who fall outside the theoretical boundaries? What if you don't meet the average life expectancy of 84.3 years for an American male who reaches age 65, or 86.6 for an

American woman who sees her 65th birthday?[3] Or, what if you live longer than this expectancy?

There are any number of projections that estimate the total amount of Social Security benefits received when taking benefits early, or at FRA, or at age 70. These projections show a "break even" point — the point at which total benefits received in all three scenarios become equal — somewhere between ages 78 and 80. People who wait to receive benefits and live considerably beyond the "break-even" point come out the big winners.

How long are you going to live?

Nobody knows. Still, knowledge of your family's longevity, as well as your personal health, is a factor in deciding whether to begin taking benefits early, or at FRA, or waiting until even later. Moreover, having additional sources of retirement income that put one in a position to not be dependent on Social Security also is a factor in the decision.

Spousal and survivor benefits

One other important thing to consider.

A person's decision on when to begin taking benefits sets a permanent level for both spousal and survivor benefits. Let's explain those briefly.

A spousal benefit is an option for a lower-earning spouse who does not have a full work history, or perhaps a reduced one. A stay-at-home parent, for instance, can at FRA be rewarded for a lifetime of hard but uncompensated work by claiming a spousal benefit generally equal to one-half of the higher-earning spouse's benefit. Such a person will receive either a spousal benefit or their own personal work-history benefit, depending on which is greater.

---

[3] Social Security Administration. "Retirement & Survivors Benefits: Life Expectancy Calculator." 2018.
https://www.ssa.gov/oact/population/longevity.html

Note here how the level of the higher earner's benefit also affects the spousal benefit. Note, too, that the maximum spousal benefit is available at FRA. Taking a spousal benefit before reaching FRA reduces its amount but waiting to take it after reaching FRA does not increase it through delayed retirement credits.

Survivor benefits also are affected by the amount of benefit being received by the deceased worker.

Beginning as early as age 60 — or age 50 for a disabled spouse — a survivor benefit can be paid to a widow or widower of a deceased worker. If the survivor waits until their FRA or later to claim the benefit, they can receive either the full benefit of the deceased spouse or their own personal benefit, whichever is greater. The lower benefit of the two disappears. (Note that a survivor benefit taken before the survivor's FRA is reduced.)

Note also that the deceased only had to be eligible for benefits, but not actually receiving them. In other words, even if the deceased had not yet begun taking benefits, the survivor is eligible to receive what the deceased would have received at FRA. But, if the deceased was receiving a reduced benefit after starting early, that reduced amount is passed on to the survivor.

Let's also note in passing that a divorced spouse also can receive a survivor benefit provided they are at least age 60; that their marriage to the deceased lasted 10 years or longer; and they have not remarried before age 60.

Again, there are hundreds of rules governing (among other things) employment income earned while receiving benefits early; survivor benefits paid to children and even elderly parents of a deceased worker; and many other special circumstances. You can't be expected to know them all. Now, I'd also like to stipulate that neither my company, The Resource Center, nor I are representatives of or affiliated with the U.S. Government or any other government agency. And a key part of Social Security is that the choice in how to take the benefits that you earned for yourself ultimately lies with you. A financial advisor, however, should have a solid understanding of the inner workings of Social Security, and you are entitled to ask about their level of knowledge when considering your choice of an advisor.

Social Security taxes

You might be surprised to learn how many people don't know that Social Security benefits can be subject to taxes. They figure that because they paid into Social Security via taxes (i.e., withholding) throughout their working years, there should be no tax when they get that money back in retirement.

Sorry to be the bearer of bad news, but it doesn't work that way for everyone.

The good news is, Social Security benefits *are not* taxable for people who fall below a certain income level, and many people in retirement fall below this limit. Moreover, benefits paid to even the richest of Americans are not fully taxed under rules in place in 2018. That's right, even Bill Gates pays taxes on no more than 85 percent of his Social Security benefits.

The key to determining Social Security taxation is a recipient's modified adjusted gross income (MAGI), also known as "provisional income." Let's define that:

Provisional income — as defined by the Internal Revenue Service includes all the components that go into determining one's adjusted gross income (AGI) on a tax return. This includes all wages, dividends, pension payments, self-employment income and taxable interest as well as all other taxable income (alimony, rental receipts, etc.).

But we're not yet done with the addition.

A Social Security recipient must also add to the AGI figure all interest and dividends from tax-free investments such as municipal bonds. Another part of the equation — and the big one for most retirees — is one half of an individual or a couple's Social Security benefits for the tax year in question.

If the resulting sum is less than $25,000 for an individual filer, or less than $32,000 for a couple filing jointly, there is no tax due on Social Security benefits. For individual filers with between $25,000 and $34,000 in provisional income, and couples filing jointly with between $32,000 and $44,000, up to 50 percent of benefits can be taxed at the filer's normal tax rate. For an individual with more than $34,000 in provisional income, and couples filing jointly with more than $44,000, up to 85 percent of benefits can be taxed at the normal rate.[4]

We'll talk in the next chapter about how provisional income and the subsequent tax on Social Security benefits can affect an individual's or a couple's overall tax picture. We'll also discuss ways of reducing provisional income.

People receiving Social Security benefits that are likely to be taxed are expected to make payments in the appropriate tax year. This can be done either through making estimated quarterly payments or by having money withheld from monthly benefits.

Wage restrictions when receiving Social Security

Let's deal with the good news first. That is, a person receiving Social Security can earn as much in wages as he or she can make by waiting until full retirement age to begin taking benefits.

Now for the bad news.

People who elect to take benefits before reaching FRA are subject to a "take-back penalty" upon exceeding a wage limit — officially known as the "earnings test annual exempt amount" — in any year prior to FRA. According to rules in place for 2018, the Social Security Administration (SSA) will take back $1 for every $2

---

[4] Social Security Administration. "Benefits Planner: Income Taxes And Your Social Security Benefit." https://www.ssa.gov/planners/taxes.html.

in wages earned above $17,020. The "take back" is typically done by withholding benefits until the penalty is paid.

The wage limit increases as one nears FRA. Beginning in January of the calendar year in which one reaches FRA, a person taking benefits early can make as much as $45,360 (in 2018) before exceeding the limit. Wages earned above that limit in the months before FRA will result in the SSA taking back $1 for every $3 earned above the limit.

A hypothetical example: Mary's FRA is age 66, but she begins taking benefits as soon as possible at age 62. She needs additional retirement income, so she returns to the workforce in a part-time job. Let's say she makes $22,000 in wages during her first year of taking benefits. Upon learning (usually from her tax return) that Mary made roughly $5,000 above the 2018 earnings limit, the SSA will withhold $2,500 — half of the excessive wages earned — from Mary's benefits. If Mary was receiving an $1,800 monthly benefit, the SSA would withhold two benefit checks ($3,600 total) to satisfy the $2,500 take-back requirement. The extra money taken — $1,100 in this case — would be returned to Mary at the start of the following year.

Note here that money taken back by the SSA is not lost forever. Upon reaching FRA, Mary will begin receiving all money taken back in the form of increased benefit payments.

Note, too, that "wages earned" means only money paid to you for employment. Regular dividends, interest, rental receipts and other types of income do not count as wages earned. Also, wages earned before a person first begins taking Social Security benefits in the middle of a year also do not count against the earnings limit. Hypothetical example: John retires in July and begins taking benefits at age 64. Wages earned prior to July do not count against his yearly earnings limit, but wages paid after that point will.

Keep in mind, too, that the SSA also can withhold benefits for a recipient who works more than 45 hours a month in self-employment.

One final note on Social Security:

Determining a Social Security claiming strategy for an individual or couple should be part of an overall retirement income plan. For such a plan to be as effective as possible, the prospective value of a Social Security benefit — whether taken early, at full retirement age or on an enhanced basis at age 70 — should be taken into consideration.

CHAPTER 4

Roadblocks of Retirement, Part 1: Taxes

In a previous chapter we talked about how knowing exactly how much income one will have in retirement — as well as understanding its sources and how long it reasonably can be expected to last — is a main factor in finding the courage to retire.

Let's now spend some time talking about balancing that retirement income against retirement expenses, both known and unforeseen. Taking a hard look at the net result of the income-vs.-outflow equation also plays an essential role in our retirement decision.

We're talking here about doing some basic budgeting, just as families do routinely during all phases of life. Retirement budgeting is only slightly different in that income is typically reduced when you stop working, even though expenses often remain the same.

In preparing any household budget you first project your monthly expenses for housing, food, utilities, insurance and other regular recurring items. You then add an allowance for irregular but common expenses such as meals and entertainment, taxes, car and home repairs, medical costs, clothing and occasional travel. Against those estimated expenses you compare your projected income from all sources: wages, Social Security (in retirement), pension or annuity income, dividends and interest, rental property income, alimony, etc.

When the accounting is done, you hope to have as much coming in as you foresee going out, or at least have the two sides be close. A lot of people preparing for retirement look at this estimated budget, like what they see, and take comfort in knowing they can afford to retire at a time of their choosing. Others see a marked imbalance on the expense side and know adjustments must be made. Occasionally, this means delaying a retirement date.

This is OK, too. Like I learned from my father, our entire lives are spent making adjustments. Life marches on in retirement, and problems will inevitably arise. But as we've done throughout our lives, we overcome, we persevere, we adapt.

This is why we'll spend the next two chapters talking about some of the financial curves and roadblocks that are unique to retirement. We'll also discuss strategies to help address these obstacles.

What are some of the expenses that might cause you to alter even the most attentive retirement income plans?

Taxes and health care —including the costs of dealing with elderly parents — are the most common. We'll address health care and long-term care in the following chapter.

Retirement taxes:
Understanding required minimum distributions

Taxes are something we deal with all our lives. For most of us, the experience began when we made just enough in a part-time job that Uncle Sam demanded his cut.

But there are some taxes that are unique to retirement. We'll talk about them here in a discussion of required minimum distributions (RMDs) and their double-whammy effect on Social Security taxes, which we touched on in the previous chapter.

The main concepts to understand about taxes in retirement are:

• The way the IRS treats retirement accounts such as your individual retirement account (IRA) or 401(k).

• How the IRS treats the taxation of your Social Security benefits, and how these can affect your overall tax picture.

Let's talk about each of those components of what I call "the retirement tax bomb."

The required minimum distribution is an amount the IRS requires you to take from "qualified" retirement accounts — that is, accounts with assets on which you have yet to pay any taxes — beginning in the year you reach age 70½.[5]

Some background here. For years during your working career, the IRS has allowed you to shelter retirement money on a tax-deferred basis in an IRA, SEP, 401(k), 403(b) or other qualified account. But you'll have to pay taxes on that money eventually; such is life in America. That time starts at age 70½ when you are required to annually withdraw a percentage of the year-end total of all your qualified retirement accounts, then pay taxes (at your normal rate) on that money you must withdraw.[6]

Your RMD is computed according to an IRS formula. The main components of the formula are the total amount of assets you have in qualified (tax-exempt) accounts, a life expectancy factor and your

---

[5] The IRS determines that you turn 70½ on the calendar date that is six months after your 70th birthday. Examples: If you turn 70 on June 30, 2017, you are deemed to be 70½ on Dec. 30, 2017. You must take your first RMD by April 1, 2018 based on the total values of qualified accounts as of Dec. 31, 2017. However, if you turn 70 on or after July 1, 2017, you are deemed to be 70½ on or after Jan. 1, 2018. You do not have to take an RMD for 2017. Your first RMD must be taken by April 1, 2019, and is based on the total value of qualified accounts in 2018. Source: "Retirement Topics: Required Minimum Distributions," www.irs.gov.

[6] The April 1 deadline to take an RMD applies only for the first year in which you are required to take a distribution. All subsequent required distributions must be taken by Dec. 31.

current age. (Note: A married couple will have separate RMDs based on the qualified accounts and age of each partner.)

The RMD amount will increase each year as the holder of the qualified accounts gets older and life expectancy decreases. As you can see, the IRS is determined to get its cut of the money you've been legally sheltering for years through tax-exempt payroll deductions to your 401(k) or annual tax-deductible contributions to your IRA. It would rather get that money while you are alive, but it will also take RMDs from your surviving spouse or heirs.

The penalty for failing to take an RMD at the required time is severe. The IRS will impose a 50 percent tax on any RMD you were supposed to take but didn't. It will impose the same penalty on any portion of an RMD you failed to take. This penalty is much more severe than the tax one would have paid on a properly taken RMD. Even the richest Americans in the highest tax bracket pay only 39 percent tax on an RMD. Moreover, it's up to you to know how much your RMD is; the IRS won't help you determine the amount.

To do this you must know how much is in all your qualified accounts at the end of a year. This is sometimes difficult to determine if you have several retirement accounts spread among several different financial advisors or brokerage firms. Each advisor will provide an annual RMD figure on the accounts they service, but it's up to you to determine the correct total of all accounts. The amount needed for the RMD does not have to be taken from each account, but it must equal the amount required for all accounts. The IRS doesn't care from which tax-deferred account or accounts you take it.[7]

---

[7] Required minimum distributions taken from a 401(k) account operate under different rules. RMDs from this account must be taken separately from those of all other qualified accounts. In other words, if you have an IRA of one or more accounts as well as an employer-sponsored plan, you must take an RMD separately from both the IRA and the employer-sponsored plan. You cannot combine the two accounts for one distribution.

Correctly determining your annual RMD number is just one reason I often urge clients with multiple retirement accounts spread among different advisors or investment firms to consolidate those accounts under one management umbrella during retirement whenever possible.

Believing as I do in "simple solutions in a complex world," I maintain that having most or all your retirement accounts – and especially your qualified, tax-deferred accounts – managed by one advisor or company is a good way to help ensure that you will take a correct RMD each year and avoid a costly penalty. Moreover, having one advisor or firm managing your retirement assets can make it easier for a surviving spouse or heirs when it comes time to deal with financial matters after your passing.

Plugging numbers into formulas

Let's look at some hypothetical examples using numbers.

Let's say you have $200,000 in one or more qualified accounts at the end of 2018. Let's also assume you turned 70½ sometime during that year. Before April 1 of 2019 you must withdraw $7,299 and pay tax on that amount at your normal tax rate. This figure, computed by the IRS RMD calculator, is based on a life expectancy factor of 27.4 and produces a required rate of distribution of 3.65 percent.[8]

Now, let's look ahead four years. You're 75 and that same $200,000 in qualified accounts now requires a $8,733 RMD based on a life expectancy factor of 22.9 years and producing a 4.37 percent required rate of distribution. This RMD number will only increase as our account holder grows older.

---

[8] The Life Expectancy Factor is a divisor established by the IRS for the purpose of determining a Required Minimum Distribution. The total account balance of a person's savings is divided by the stipulated life expectancy factor on the IRS Uniform Lifetime Table. The life expectancy factor varies by age, beginning at age 70.

Now, let's look at what happens if our account holder fails to take this first RMD or takes an incorrect number. Let's say he knows nothing of this requirement and fails to take any RMD when first required to do so. He was obligated to take $7,299, and because he is in a 22 percent tax bracket — one of the new tax brackets created by the Tax Cuts and Jobs Act of 2017 — he would pay a tax of about $1,605 on that distribution. But in failing to take the RMD, he must instead pay a 50 percent tax/penalty of $3,650 — half of the amount he should have taken in a required distribution.

What if he took some but not all of the required $7,299?

Let's say he forgot to add in a qualified account stashed somewhere and took only $5,000, paying a 22 percent tax of $1,100 on that amount. The IRS would likely see an unclaimed balance of roughly $2,300 and charge an additional tax/penalty of $1,150 — again, half of the unclaimed balance. That would bring his total RMD taxes for that year to $2,250, considerably more than the $1,605 he would have paid had he done everything correctly.

Let's note here that a person is welcome to take more than is required in an annual RMD. Just make darn sure you don't take less.

The impact of RMDs

The tax impact of RMDs comes in several areas.

While many people plan to start taking income from tax-deferred retirement accounts at age 70, some don't. Perhaps these fortunate folks are doing well enough financially through wages, Social Security, dividends and income and possibly a pension that they don't want or need money from an IRA. Being forced to take money from such accounts through an RMD represents little more than an additional tax burden, one that may elevate them into a higher tax bracket. Increased taxes are something you dearly want to avoid in retirement, even more than you did in your working years.

This is because, when we are working, we reluctantly accept higher taxes as a natural byproduct of receiving raises or taking better-paying jobs. In retirement, however, our income becomes relatively fixed and is more likely to experience dips than raises. Any rise in expenses, such as taxes, becomes a drain on spending power.

Let's also look at the impact of RMDs and their corresponding taxes on a surviving spouse or heirs.

A married couple typically deals with its tax obligations with the help of at least two standard deductions, the value of which were doubled following the elimination of personal exemptions in the 2017 tax reform bill. But when the kids are gone and one spouse passes, the survivor suddenly faces the same tax obligation but now with only one standard deduction to offset the load. Beyond that, the survivor also loses one of the two Social Security benefits – the smaller of the two – that contributed to the couple's income. And even as all this is happening, the RMDs required on any tax-deferred accounts left behind by the departed spouse continue to increase as the widow or widower grows older.

There is an impact on the couple's heirs, as well. While the surviving spouse is likely to get the first tax obligation left behind in the dearly departed's IRA, that obligation will fall to the couple's children or other beneficiaries when the surviving spouse passes with untaxed money remaining in an IRA. In my experience, most heirs take that money in a lump sum, pay the taxes owed in the first year, then spend much of that reduced inheritance within a year or two.

There are, however, ways to diffuse this tax burden on surviving spouses and heirs, and we'll discuss these concepts shortly.

But let's look first at one more reason you'll want to keep a lid on your RMDs and their resulting taxes. I'm talking here about the potential double whammy effect of RMDs on your Social Security benefits.

Provisional income and Social Security taxes

We addressed in Chapter 3 the components of provisional income and how its different levels determine what percentage of your Social Security benefits are taxed.

As a review, let's note quickly that provisional income is determined by combining all regular components of adjusted gross income and one half of Social Security benefits, as well as any tax-free interest. Let's also note that many people in the early stages of retirement pay no taxes at all on Social Security. Because their wage income is eliminated or greatly reduced when they stop working full time, many people find their provisional income falls below the $25,00 level at which an individual filer begins paying tax on benefits, or below the $32,000 level at which a couple filing jointly will have benefits taxed according to IRS regulations in 2018.

But then, at age 70½, the RMD rules kick in, and some of these same people suddenly find themselves facing a new tax situation.

Taking required distributions and paying tax on previously untaxed money not only immediately increases one's tax bill, but it also increases provisional income — possibly to the point that taxation of Social Security benefits will be affected. This new income might raise an individual's provisional income level into the $25,000 to $34,000 range, at which up to 50 percent of benefits are subject to tax at the individual filer's normal tax rate. For a couple filing jointly, a rise into the provisional income range of $32,000 to $44,000 means up to 50 percent of benefits can be taxed.

Don't forget, either, that individuals making more than $34,000 and couples topping $44,000 in provisional income can see up to 85 percent of their benefits taxed.

This is why I can't emphasize enough the importance of trying to limit the double-whammy impact of RMDs in retirement.

Defuse the "tax bomb": Roth IRA conversions

Among the strategies used to reduce the tax impact of RMDs is the Roth IRA conversion, which can lower the amount of tax-deferred money prior to the time of mandatory distributions.

Many people know at least something of the Roth conversion, but may not fully grasp all the details. They likely know that a Roth IRA is funded by money that already has been taxed, making it different from a regular IRA, 401(k) or 403(b) account comprised of money still waiting to be taxed. Some may know that Roth IRA money is not subject to required distributions during the lifetime of the account holder, and that qualified distributions can be taken without tax obligations as long as certain conditions are met.[9] Many also know that Roth funds can be passed on to heirs without tax obligations.

There is much to be said for building up Roth IRA accounts as a source of tax-free income in retirement. But for many people, there are just as many reasons why they avoid doing so.

The idea of paying taxes is the biggest drawback.

In our working years, when we have young families still and every dollar is needed for routine living expenses, we view contributions to our retirement savings primarily through the lens of a tax incentive. Payroll contributions to a company-sponsored 401(k) are made on a pre-tax basis; that is, this money is shielded from taxation (for a while, at least). Contributions to a traditional IRA usually are made with the same tax-saving consideration.

---

[9] Qualified distributions from Roth accounts can be tax-free if taken a) after a 5-year period that begins in the first year a Roth contribution is made on your behalf; b) on any distribution after you reach age 59½; c) on any distribution made to your beneficiary or your estate after your death; and d) for a purpose that meets the requirements of "first home exceptions." Source: Publication 590-B, "Distributions from Individual Retirement Arrangements," www.irs.gov.

As we approach or enter retirement, however, that view on taxes needs to be re-evaluated. That growing pool of tax-deferred retirement money is going to be taxed eventually, and that time is coming sooner than later. The "pay me now or pay me later" dilemma enters the picture.

This is when people may want to consider moving some funds from their tax-deferred IRA accounts into a Roth account. Yes, you will pay taxes now (at your normal tax rate) on any funds you move out of an IRA or a 401(k). But, you're eventually going to pay those taxes anyway, so why not consider doing so in the final years of full-time employment when income is still incoming, or early in retirement when your overall tax bill may be lower?

This is the time you may want to visit with your financial advisor and tax specialist or accountant to determine if you can afford to move some tax-deferred funds into a more tax-advantageous Roth. You pay some additional tax now, but the money moved into the Roth will continue to grow until you choose to take tax-free distributions on your own terms. (Note, income from a Roth IRA is non-taxable, assuming you take distributions after your age 59½ and the account has been open for at least five years). Equally important, Roth distributions *do not* contribute to your provisional income that affects Social Security taxation. Moreover, Roth money can survive you and be passed on to a surviving spouse or heirs on a non-taxable basis if some simple conditions are met.

Roth conversions can be made in a lump sum but are generally done over a period of years.

As a hypothetical, let's say you've got $250,000 in IRA money — perhaps from a rollover of your company-sponsored 401(k) into your personally controlled IRA. You are now age 62, and you learn that, at age 70½, you must begin taking taxable required distributions from that pool. Is it in your interest to slowly begin draining that pool, perhaps by $15,000 a year, so that over the next eight years until you reach 70½, your $250,000 pool is reduced by $120,000 to $130,000?

To help illustrate the impact, consider that the first-year RMD for a person turning 70½ in 2017 with a $250,000 IRA is $7,299, which would generate a $1,605 tax bill for a person in a 22 percent tax bracket. By contrast, a $130,000 IRA for the same person would require only a $4,744 RMD with an $1,043 first-year tax tab for that same person in the 22 percent tax bracket.

One other consideration: After making a choice to fund a Roth, you also must choose the mechanism for growing the funds within it.

Any financial tool available for your IRA or brokerage account can also be employed within a Roth, assuming the account administrator or issuer permits it. You might purchase the kind of principally protected annuity we'll assess in more detail in an upcoming chapter, or take as much risk as you can stomach on the stock market. Bottom line, money in a Roth has all the allocation options available anywhere else.

Stretching out the "tax bomb"

What happens when you die with tax-deferred money remaining in an IRA?

Well, someone (or several someones) will inherit that money and the tax obligation that goes with it. However, at the time of the completion of this book in 2018, there were still options available to ease that tax burden on your heirs.[10] One of the more popular options is the "stretch IRA" that can help an inherited IRA last for years while setting up a more comfortable tax structure for the inheritors.

---

[10] Eliminating, or at least changing, the stretch IRA had been suggested in previous presidential administrations, including as recently as the Obama administration.

Let's begin our examination of the stretch IRA concept by looking first at what typically happens with an inherited IRA.

Whether a surviving spouse is required to take RMDs from the IRA of a deceased spouse depends on the age of the deceased, the age of the survivor, and whether RMDs were already being taken on the original IRA. In some cases, the surviving spouse can roll the original IRA into their own personal IRA and delay taking RMDs until the survivor reaches 70½. In other situations, an inheriting spouse may have to take RMDs if the deceased was already doing so. The options facing a surviving spouse can be complicated, so it is best to consult with your financial advisor before making a decision on what to do with an IRA you either inherit or receive as a beneficiary.

When the surviving spouse eventually passes, a non-spouse beneficiary (or more than one) will inherit the original IRA. This person or persons has several options:

• Take the money in a lump sum distribution and pay taxes on that entire amount immediately.

• Take the entire amount over the course of a 5-year period, paying taxes annually only on the amount taken. A minimum distribution is required each year, but the beneficiary can also take more than the RMD until the account is depleted.

• Take the money through annual RMDs on a "stretch basis" over the course of the beneficiary's life expectancy. The new RMD is calculated based on the typically younger age of the new beneficiary, meaning their share of the inherited IRA is likely to grow and last over a longer period.

That last stretch option exists for several people over the life of the IRA. A hypothetical example:

The original owner, knowing a spouse is well-provided-for without the assets of his or her IRA, might designate that a tax-heavy IRA skip a generation and be passed directly to children or grandchildren. The advantage here is these younger heirs, while required to take minimum distributions as non-spouse beneficiaries, will have their RMDs determined by their ages, not that of the original IRA owner. Their required distributions will be decreased, and so is the tax obligation.

This, in theory, should allow the original IRA to grow and retain funds for a longer period. Also, an older grandchild might receive income in their late teens or early 20s while in a low tax bracket. That RMD will increase each year as the beneficiary ages until the money in the original IRA is depleted.

The stretch IRA, in summary, provides a way to allow heirs who inherit your IRA or other taxable assets to stretch out the required distributions and tax obligations over longer periods of time, taking smaller bites each year rather than a big gulp all at once. People approaching or in retirement who are looking for ways to provide for heirs are well advised to at least discuss the stretch concept with their financial advisor.

Staying ahead of the RMD drain

But enough discussion of RMD negatives. Let's look instead at a more uplifting prospect of growing one's IRA accounts — for at least a few years.

We know the prospect of outliving our money is one of the biggest fears many people face in retirement. We also know conventional wisdom suggests, once the IRS requires us to begin taking mandatory distributions from our tax-deferred savings, those accounts can be reduced significantly over time. For retirees who choose to keep IRA money in cash or other investments with little prospect for growth, the chance of someday seeing an IRA account drained completely is very real.

At the same time, however, you should also be aware that when your IRA money is maintained in principally protected financial vehicles with the prospect for crediting interest, while not guaranteed, one might experience account growth that keeps pace with, or even exceeds, the rate of RMDs for at least a period of time.

You already know I'm a big fan of fixed index annuities when they make sense for a client's situation. Part of the reason for that affinity is because I've seen what they can do in maintaining and in some instances even growing IRA accounts that are subject to RMDs. Every situation is unique, of course, but on more than one occasion I have actually seen IRA accounts grow despite RMD deductions.

This pattern doesn't last forever, needless to say. Eventually the ever-growing rate of required annual distribution rises to a point where it exceeds what one might reasonably expect in a typical rate of return on a conservative financial product. This generally happens somewhere around age 83 when an RMD rate of 6.14 percent could potentially exceed a hypothetical interest crediting rate of 4 to 6 percent.

Even so, think about what you might accomplish in growing an IRA as fast or faster than the IRS can drain it over, say, a 13-year period from age 70½ through 83.

You are effectively extending the overall longevity of the IRA, which in turn can help ease some of the fear about running out of money as you get further into retirement. Beyond that, by supplementing your Social Security, pension and other income with required distributions from qualified, tax-deferred accounts, you may find you must draw less income from your non-qualified accounts, thus giving them the chance to continue to grow.

Another hypothetical example: Say you've got a qualified, tax-deferred IRA account invested in a fixed index annuity that averaged an annual growth of between 4 and 6 percent while protecting against the loss of principal. At age 70½, the IRS will start taking an RMD from that account at a rate of 3.65 percent. In theory and in practice, that account is experiencing a slight growth despite distributions being taken. At age 75 the rate of distribution grows to 4.37 percent, and now your account is holding the line at best. At age 83, however, that mandatory distribution rate has increased to 6.14 percent, and now the IRS is likely taking out more than you can reasonably expect to make in growth. Remember, too, this IRS cut is only going to get bigger the longer you live.

Still, until this point, you've used account growth to effectively counterbalance the account drain of RMDs. I'm not saying your IRA balance at age 83 will be the same as when you started taking RMDs at age 70½, but for some people, depending how you invest, it could be close. I'm also not suggesting that the IRA portion of your retirement savings won't be depleted by, say, age 95.

Still, given that a goal in retirement is to maintain your savings for as long as one can, this strategy is one that can help accomplish that goal. You have the potential to stretch the life expectancy of an IRA, help reduce the drain on other accounts that aren't subject to RMDs, and hopefully help remove some of the stress that goes with wondering if you will live longer than your money will.

Keep in mind that the stretch IRA is just a strategy and there is no guarantee that it will extend the life of an IRA that is subject to RMDs.

The Joneses did more than just keep up

Bob and Carol Jones were real clients to whom I've given fictional names. I first met them when Bob was 80, about nine years after he first began taking RMDs on his IRA.

Bob and Carol had done well for themselves in their working years. But after nine years of taking RMDs, their retirement nest egg was at around $611,000. Anticipating that assisted living might be in their near future — and it was eventually — and knowing how expensive that would be, Bob and Carol came to me worried that they might run out of money.

Their retirement account was split almost equally between an IRA (upon which they owed taxes when taking required distributions) and a non-qualified account upon which they already were paying taxes on capital gains, dividends and interest. Their IRA was invested mainly in cash and bank CDs that offered little room for growth.

For a situation such as Bob and Carol's, where a couple is well into retirement, one strategy I might suggest they consider is restructuring a portion of both accounts, allotting more of both qualified and non-qualified accounts to indexed annuities to have modest growth potential with some protection from market loss. In doing so, the client would continue taking income from the IRA — of course, for someone in Bob and Carol's situation, they would have to as they are over 70½ — while leaving assets in their non-qualified account relatively untouched, growing and held in reserve for future needs. Keep in mind, too, that even as we are taking RMD income from the IRA, some of the money going out for income is being partially replaced by index credited interest in the fixed index annuity.

Now, for Bob and Carol's specific scenario, Carol's life changed 13 years later when Bob died at age 93, leaving Carol, 91, with total control of the nest egg. She was then faced with the loss of both Bob's pension and the spousal Social Security check, while still needing about the same amount of income for her living expenses as before Bob's death. Additionally, Carol was now a single filer for tax purposes, and, as the surviving spouse, was more likely to need nursing home care.

Bob and Carol's situation is in no way unique; for many, many couples, these are the realities the surviving spouse, usually the wife, will face. At this point, we usually focus more on income. The difference a widow needs to make up in income is typically more than what can be offset by growth in a retirement nest egg. Thankfully, with a bit of foresight, we can see this situation coming a few decades in advance and plan for it. For these situations, we often begin taking more income from the non-qualified account that was hopefully allowed to grow in this period, while being aware that, by age 90, RMDs from qualified accounts are up in the 9 percent range, which can drain an IRA pretty quickly during bad market stretches. The main thing is by planning ahead and structuring retirement savings years earlier, we can provide ourselves with a better prospect of living as long as our money.

CHAPTER 5

Roadblocks of Retirement, Part 2: Health Care

I t's probably the second-biggest concern I hear from people either approaching or just entering retirement. It's a concern I rank behind only "I'm afraid of living longer than my money will" on any Top 10 litany of retirement fears.

It's a concern expressed in different ways, but all have a common theme:

How will I handle a major illness or long-term medical condition in retirement? What will I do if I become physically or mentally disabled and need extended nursing care on either an at-home or assisted living basis? What can I do to avoid becoming an emotional and financial burden on my loved ones who might become my caregivers?

Well, you have a reason to be concerned, as health care typically represents the single largest drain on a retirement nest egg.

According to the 2018 Retiree Health Care Cost Estimate prepared by Fidelity Investments, a married couple receiving Medicare coverage at age 65 might expect to spend some $280,000 on health care over the remainder of their lives.[11] This estimate includes Medicare payments for Parts B and D coverage (which we will discuss following); premiums for Medicare supplemental insurance that covers some or all of Part B expenses not covered by Medicare (another topic featured elsewhere in this chapter); as well as deductibles, co-payments and other out-of-pocket costs for services not covered by Medicare, such as dentistry, eye care and hearing aids.

These projected costs only multiply, mind you, when nursing home expenses are factored in, which they are not in the preceding figure.

Let's make note of a couple things here before moving on.

Note that the preceding projected costs were for a couple free of chronic disease. The onset of cancer, stroke, heart disease, diabetes, dementia — just to name a few of the diseases common in retirement — will significantly increase these estimates.

Establishing the financial means to meet this kind of expense is a huge factor in finding the courage to retire.

Granted, some people will be fortunate enough to live large portions of their lives without incurring large medical or nursing care expenses. Congratulations to them, and here's wishing that all of you can follow in their footsteps. At the same time, however, it's a simple fact of life that we all will eventually become less healthy as we get older and the human body begins to deteriorate.

How many times have you heard someone say, "If I'd have known I was going to live this long, I would have taken better care of myself"? Well, sure, there are things we can do to improve our chances of living a longer, healthier life. We can exercise, avoid smoking, reduce stress, watch what we eat and drink. But even as we

---

[11] Elizabeth O'Brien. Time Magazine. April 19, 2018. "Here's How Much theAverage Couple Will Spend on Health Care Costs in Retirement." http://time.com/money/5246882/heres-how-much-the-average-couple-will-

attempt preventative measures, we are often limited in what we can do to ward off the debilitating effects of, say, a stroke or the onset of dementia.

Here's another sad fact of life: The cost of health care is only going to increase as our American population ages and the demand for elder care services grows. The baby boomers who were the biggest part of our expanding population in the late 40s, 50s and 60s are now entering retirement age and needing more health care than ever. Advances in medicine and pharmaceuticals may prolong our life expectancy, but they do so at an increasing cost.

How does one budget for that kind of rising expense?

Well, budgeting is all about planning, and planning for health care expenses in retirement involves planning to live a long time, even longer than you might reasonably expect. This is planning that needs to be done while you are still able to do it, when the prospect of a life-changing health crisis is just a possibility as opposed to a harsh reality. This is planning that should be done while you are still able to make good decisions about providing for medical or nursing costs that will affect not only your own retirement savings but possibly also the finances of loved ones who might become a big part of your caregiver team.

Again, there is not much one can do to completely eliminate all the emotional and physical strain caregivers experience when watching a parent or older loved one going through a life-changing medical event. There are, however, things you can do in advance of that time that can at least minimize some of the financial strain that typically accompanies long-term care. Preparing to handle the "what ifs" of health care is a huge part of planning for retirement. The sooner you begin this planning process, the more options you will find available.

My company, The Resource Center, has positioned itself to assist people in this planning process. We'll be talking later in this chapter about various ways of providing for long-term care, whether through personally funded investment planning, the purchase of insurance products, or through estate planning options. We'll also examine health care coverage for seniors. We'll spend some time on the basics of Medicare, the government health care program that takes effect at age 65. We'll also take a brief look at how Medicaid — a program of federal and state government health care assistance for people with limited assets or low income — can be used in funding nursing home care.

But, before we start looking at ways of dealing with the problems retirees face, let's look first at the everyday battle faced by their children, relatives or even close friends who often become caregivers.

The hidden costs of caring for aging parents

As I mentioned in Chapter 1, I learned firsthand about the mental, physical and financial strains a family can experience during a long-term health care crisis when my father's life — as well as that of our family — changed dramatically after his first heart attack at the way-too-young age of 38.

Later in my professional career, I began to more fully understand the hidden costs incurred by families who care for aging parents. Not only were there the financial strains of paying for nursing care, but also the mental fatigue, the stress and frustration that comes with watching one's elderly parents essentially become children once again. I quickly saw how caring for older loved ones with physical disabilities or mental incapacity took a heavy toll on younger caregivers who give up family time, income and work tenure.

I especially remember the case of one woman in particular.

Shannon — once again, a fictional name for a real person — had a father who had been battling Parkinson's disease for years.

Dementia ultimately entered the picture, and over time he no longer could bathe or take care of himself.

Shannon's father and mother eventually moved to her Missouri community to be closer to family. Trying to help her father avoid the nursing home confinement he needed but resisted, Shannon threw herself into doing everything she could to support her parents.

Though she also had her own family to care for, Shannon eventually left full-time employment to become a nearly full-time caregiver for her parents. She was giving up more than just her time. In putting her career on hold, she not only was forfeiting about $3,000 in monthly income but also job tenure and growth of her own Social Security pool. At one time, she and her parents discussed the prospect of them paying her $3,000 a month to recoup part of what she was losing in wages, but it soon became apparent that her folks could barely afford $1,000 a month for this alternative to nursing home care.

Shannon's situation is a perfect illustration of the hidden cost of senior health care. It also illustrates the need to plan for the health care costs we are likely to encounter in retirement — not just for ourselves, but the hidden costs our loved ones are likely to encounter.

Let's look now at some different ways to do that via three general strategies: financial planning, insurance options and estate planning.

Financing your retirement health care: Financial planning options

One of the simplest ways to provide funds for long-term medical or nursing care in retirement is a do-it-yourself system in which you earmark a significant part of your retirement savings specifically for this purpose.

How much of your retirement money should you hold in reserve for future health or nursing care? At the minimum, one should plan to provide for an average of projected expenses.

According to LongTermCare.gov, about two-thirds of today's 65-year-olds will need long-term care support services of some kind, while about 20 percent will need care for more than five years.[12]

The annual cost of nursing home care can be eye-popping. According to the 2015 Cost of Care Survey reported by SeniorHomes.com, the national average for a private room in a nursing home was $250 a day, or $91,250 annually. The national average for a semi-private room in a nursing home was $220 a day, or $80,300 annually.[13]

Missouri residents may fare slightly better. A 2017 Cost of Care Survey cited by LendingAgeMissouri.org reported the median cost of a private room in a Missouri nursing home to be $65,700 annually. The median cost for a semi-private room in a Missouri nursing home was reported as $58,948 annually.[14]

Missouri, it should be noted, has one of the nation's lowest median nursing home costs. Even so, using the figures for the median cost of a semi-private room in Missouri and anticipating three years of possible nursing home care, one might anticipate the need to earmark some $177,000 of retirement savings to cover such care. This is money in current investment assets or funds that might be realized from noninvestment assets such as the sale or downsizing of a home.

---

[12] LongTermCare.gov. 2018. "How Much Care Will You Need?" https://longtermcare.acl.gov/the-basics/how-much-care-will-you-need.html.
[13] Sara Shelton and Andrea Watts. SeniorHomes.com. 2018. "Nursing Home Costs." www.seniorhomes.com/p/nursing-home-cost
[14] Leading Age Missouri. 2017. "The Cost of Care." www.leadingagemissouri.org/page/Cost?&hhsearchterms="cost+and+care"

If you hope to finance long-term care from your retirement portfolio, the idea of having sustainable retirement income — that is, money you cannot outlive, such as that provided by a fixed index annuity — is especially important. This is because, when you or your loved ones are looking for ways to pay expenses associated with nursing care, you can't afford to have a substantial portion of your income be dependent on the rise and fall of market-based investments.

One might also consider the option of a Health Savings Account. These are typically established during your working years as enrollment is not available to people receiving Medicare.[15]

In broad-stroke terms, an HSA allows eligible persons — those who have what the IRS designates as a High Deductible Health Plan— the option to take a yearly tax deduction on contributions to an HSA account.16 Moreover, any employer contributions to an HSA do not count as taxable income. The HSA account grows over the years until you take distributions, which are not taxed when taken for an eligible medical expense.[17] Long-term care and nursing home costs are among eligible expenses.

---

[15] You are ineligible to enroll in an HSA once you enroll in Medicare. You can, however, take distributions from your previously established HSA after starting Medicare. Merely being old enough (age 65) for Medicare does not make you ineligible for an HSA should you still be working and enrolled in a high-deductible employer-provided health care plan. Also, a person might qualify for an Medicare Advantage Medical Savings Account (MSA) if enrolled in a Medicare Advantage plan with a qualifying high deductible.

[16] The minimum contribution necessary to qualify for an HSA in 2017 was $1,350 for an individual and $2,700 for a married couple. The maximum HSA contribution in 2017 was $3,450 for an individual and $6,900 for a couple. Persons age 55 and older can make an additional $1,000 annual "catch up" contribution.

[17] Any distribution taken from an HSA used for a non-medical purpose can be taxed as regular income with a 10 percent tax penalty.

HSA plans can be helpful for a family's current and long-term health care concerns, but they also can be complicated. Discussing your options with a qualified professional is encouraged here.

Insurance solutions

Insurance-based products continue to provide a hedge against the costs of long-term care during retirement, but even these products have changed over time. It used to be that long-term care insurance represented the gold standard of coverage, but other insurance products now offer a cost-favorable alternative.

Companies still sell long-term care insurance policies, but they can be expensive. How expensive? Well, let's look at some examples.

In all the following examples, the person seeking coverage qualifies medically for a $150 daily benefit after a 90-day waiting period with a five-year qualified benefit. The chart below shows a sample cost of long-term care insurance for both men and women of differing ages. Note in all examples how the cost of coverage increases as your age does.[18]

Age 50

Male — approximately $1,500-$1,600 annual premium
Female — approximately $2,400-$2,500 annual premium

Age 60

Male — approximately $2,000-$2,100 annual premium
Female — approximately $2,900-$3,000 annual premium

[18] Figures provided do not necessarily reflect a substantial survey of all products available.

Age 70

Male — approximately $3,000-$3,100 annual premium

Female — approximately $5,000-$5,100 annual premium

Note here the preceding chart reflects only the initial premium paid at the time of issue at different ages in life. That premium may or may not hold firm over the life of the contract prior to using the benefit. Some companies may hold that premium price firm; others may increase the premium over time. A person considering long-term care insurance should be aware of the insurance company's history regarding premium increases.

Note also, because long-term care coverage is a use-it-or-lose-it proposition, coverage purchased through previous payments will be lost once you stop making payments. There are options to purchase return-of-premium policies, but these tend to be quite expensive — often to the point of doubling the annual premium.

But there are other insurance-related options available for long-term health needs.

Many life insurance policies today offer "living benefits riders" that allow the insured to take money from the policy's death benefit to use for long-term care. Similarly, some of today's annuities also offer living benefits that allow the contract holder to use a percentage of the contract's cash value each year for long-term care.

Keep in mind that using life insurance and annuity contracts to help cover the costs associated with long-term health needs will reduce other available benefits of the policy, such as the death benefit to heirs. However, it does provide an alternative strategy to traditional long-term care insurance.

Life insurance? At my age?

Now, I can almost sense what you're thinking at this point — mainly because I've heard the sentiment expressed on many occasions.

I'm either now retired or soon about to be, you're saying. Why do I need life insurance at this advanced time of my life? Sure, it made sense when I was a younger worker with a young family that needed protection if something real bad happened to me. But now I'm looking down the barrel at age 70, and you're talking to me about life insurance?

It's a reasonable argument. But so too are the arguments in favor of maintaining a life insurance policy with living benefits in retirement. Let's look at an example.

I often talk to clients who wonder what to do with required minimum distributions they have to take but don't necessarily need for income at age 70½. They can, of course, invest this money; spend it on a cruise or a bass boat or some other retirement dream; give it to their kids or a charity; or play it all on red in Vegas should they choose to do so (though this clearly is not a recommendation). Another option: They can use this money as premiums on a universal life insurance policy with living benefits that will provide them funds for future long-term care.

As a hypothetical example, let's say they purchase a universal life policy using $10,000 a year in RMD money to pay premiums for 10 years before cutting off the payments. At the end of that 10-year period they've made premium payments of $100,000 in a policy that now has a $250,000 death benefit. Assuming the policy can sustain itself and not lapse, that's a quarter million-dollar tax-free death benefit to beneficiaries. Better yet, the policy could potentially produce income that can be used while the insured is still alive. Assuming the policy has a living benefits rider, if the insured needs long-term nursing care, they can sometimes take up to half of that death benefit to help pay for that care. Anything not used for long-term care remains available as a death benefit.

Granted, the drawback here is that you are paying life insurance premiums at a time later in life when you thought you were finished with such purchases. But look at it another way. You are continuing to invest in your heirs and beneficiaries, as well as in yourself or a spouse in providing a funding source for long-term care.

The primary purpose of purchasing life insurance must always be for the death benefit and the policy involves costs and restrictions for providing this benefit, which include a surrender charge for early withdrawals.[19] You will also need to qualify for insurance through the medical underwriting process. However, in addition to providing an asset for the loved ones you leave behind, it may also provide a cost-effective means to help cover the long-term health care costs that may otherwise decrease your liquid assets. Using living benefits from a life insurance policy helps protect your other assets and possibly replenishes to your estate the premiums paid over the years to provide the benefits.

Think about it. This is an insurance policy that provides a significant tax-free death benefit when you die. It may also provide money when needed for long-term care costs and may leave a remaining death benefit — remember, the benefits you use in life are taken from the death benefit — that may well be equal to the premiums you paid over the years.

In my mind, these aspects of today's life insurance policies make them well worth your consideration even at an age when you thought you no longer needed life insurance. While the benefits seem obvious, there are aspects of these policies that can be

---

[19] Policy loans and withdrawals will reduce available cash values and death benefits and may cause the policy to lapse or affect any guarantees against lapse. Additional premium payments may be required to keep the policy in force.

complicated, meaning you should consult an insurance professional well versed in these kinds of coverages.

Keep in mind that for all life insurance policies, the contractual guarantees are only as strong as the insurance company that sells the product. Living benefits are available in the form of accelerated death benefits. These benefits *are not* a replacement for long-term care (LTC) insurance. Living benefits and LTC riders are not available on all index universal life products and may not be available in all states. It's important to remember that policyholders may have to meet minimum eligibility requirements if they want to add accelerated death benefits or LTC riders to their policies, and those added benefits typically come with a fee.

Long-term care provisions of annuities

Let's look at another option for funding long-term care provided through the living benefits riders available (sometimes for an additional fee) in some annuities. There are many annuities today that, either through a rider or a base contract feature, allow for the acceleration of the income account value of the annuity to be used in qualifying situations to help cover the costs associated with long-term care. In some instances, it may even allow for 100 percent liquidation without penalty if used for a terminal illness.

I talked recently with some clients who wondered how they would afford the "what ifs" of retirement. They had some $300,000 in bank accounts and various CDs. They had no plans to touch that principal (through using the interest payments for income) as it was their hedge against future long-term health care. That's when we started talking about alternative funding for medical care or potential nursing home costs. They said they had good Medicare Supplemental insurance — which we'll address in more detail later in this chapter — that would pay most of what Medicare did not cover. That was excellent news; their future medical costs were covered.

We then talked about converting a portion of their money-market assets — which were paying less than 1 percent interest in the low-interest post-Recession environment — into an indexed annuity. This contract gave them access to their premium — 100 percent access after three years — when used for qualified long-term care expenses.

This is just one example of what a long-term care rider or home health care rider on an annuity may provide. While these riders are commonly available on fixed index annuities, each policy is different and may provide different benefits or have different requirements or exclusions.

Estate planning solutions

Many people concerned about spending much or all their retirement savings on long-term care consider the prospect of using Medicaid — government health care assistance for Americans with low incomes — as a supplemental source of paying for such care.

To qualify for Medicaid assistance, however, an applicant must demonstrate that they have only a few allowable assets. (We will discuss the limits on those assets in greater detail later in this chapter in the section on "Understanding Medicaid assistance for long-term care.") Any assets exceeding the allowable can disqualify someone from receiving Medicaid assistance.

Moreover, the Medicaid qualification process involves a five-year "look back" to assure that an applicant owned only the allowable assets during the previous 60 months.

Some people attempt to satisfy this "look back" requirement using an estate planning strategy generically known as an asset protection trust.

In its most elemental form, this is an irrevocable trust that protects assets from the claims of creditors. Because Medicaid is essentially regarded as a creditor, assets included in such a trust are not "countable" in the process by which Medicaid determines if a person is eligible for financial assistance. Again, keep in mind that assets must be transferred into this trust at least 60 months prior to applying for Medicaid assistance.

The process of establishing this trust can be complicated and it certainly requires the assistance of an estate planning attorney. Moreover, the trust has limitations in that the trustee — usually a spouse or children of the person needing nursing care — often may have only limited control of the assets. Attorneys with whom I work closely have told me that when they explain the complexity of transferring assets for Medicaid qualification — to say nothing of the annual administration of an asset protection trust that must file its own tax return each year — people who express interest in qualifying often become discouraged and seek alternative financial solutions.

We'll take a more detailed look at estate planning in the following chapter.

Understanding the basics of Medicare

An entire book can be written on the subject of Medicare as well as the implications of Medicaid in retirement. I don't intend to write that book here.

At the same time, however, no discussion of health care in retirement is complete without some understanding of the basics of Medicare, the government program that provides health insurance for Americans age 65 and older.

In a similar vein, retirees also should have a basic understanding of Medicaid, the government program providing health care for people with low incomes, which also is used by many seniors to assist with nursing home expenses.

Understanding the basics of both programs is another step in reducing the fear many retirees have about running out of money. First, you should understand that Medicare was designed to cover acute medical care as opposed to long-term care. It will cover some rehabilitation costs, but Medicare does not cover long-term nursing care. This is why we spent most of this chapter talking about the need to plan in advance for long-term care in retirement. Medicare has several different basic components.

Part A is coverage that applies when you are an "admitted" patient in the hospital as determined medically necessary by your primary care physician. You automatically enroll in Part A at age 65, or if you have been on Social Security disability for 24 months. The premium for this coverage has been paid through tax withholding throughout your working years.

Note that there is a deductible on hospital admittance that covers a period of the first 60 days. Another deductible goes into effect beginning on day 61. Consequently, a person using basic Medicare only could incur multiple deductibles depending on the length of their hospital stay and the number of admittances annually. Because of the potential cost of these deductibles, a Medicare supplemental plan that pays some or even all of what Medicare does not can be very important when planning for health care costs in retirement.

(We'll take a closer look at Medicare supplement plans later in this chapter.).

Part A will also cover medically necessary rehabilitation in a skilled nursing facility after you have been "admitted" to a hospital for a minimum of three days. Medicare defines "three-day admittance" as being three "midnight" stays.

The number of days covered for skilled rehabilitation is limited to your daily improvement as determined by the therapist. Part A also covers some home health care visits, provided they are deemed to be medically necessary.

Part B covers outpatient costs that include (but are not limited to) doctor visits, diagnostic testing, X-rays, laboratory expenses, hospital observation and certain durable medical devices. There is an annual deductible that can change from year to year. After the annual deductible is met, Medicare then covers 80 percent of outpatient costs, meaning your share is 20 percent. There is no maximum out-of-pocket limit in Part B, meaning that depending on the seriousness of your health condition and the extent of your treatment, your costs could be financially devastating. Again, this reinforces the need for Medicare supplemental insurance, which we describe below.

There is a premium to be paid for Part B coverage. It can vary annually or depend on your income. This premium is usually deducted monthly from your Social Security benefit, but also can be paid directly if you are not yet receiving Social Security benefits but still want to receive Part B coverage. As with Part A you are eligible for Part B coverage at age 65 or if you have been on Social Security disability for 24 months.

Enrollment in Part B is not required if you have "credible coverage" — such as that provided by an employer's group health care plan to people who continue to work beyond age 65 — that is at least equal to what Part B covers. However, if you don't enroll in Part B when you are first eligible and can't provide proof of credible coverage during the time you were not enrolled, there is a penalty due should you ultimately opt for late enrollment. This is a penalty added on to your Part B premium for the rest of your life and is based on the amount of time you were eligible for enrollment but opted not to participate. (See the Chapter 8 "common mistakes" section on "Opting out of Part B coverage.")

Prescription drug coverage

Basic Medicare provides no prescription drug coverage, but Medicare has appointed several insurance companies to provide such coverage on its behalf. In what is commonly known as Medicare Part D, Medicare establishes basic coverage requirements that these companies must follow.

Drugs are arranged in tiers, and the price you will pay typically depends on the tier level of the prescription. Tier 1 includes the most common generic drugs. Tier 2 features less common generics. Tier 3 includes most common brand-name drugs, with the highest-cost brand-name drugs being found in Tier 4.

Some Part D plans have a deductible on all tiers, while others have a deductible only on Tiers 3 and 4. Some plans have no deductible. As with Part B, if you don't enroll in Part D when first eligible or present proof of "credible coverage," there is a continuing penalty for life once you do enroll. As these plans all have different coverage, the most important thing to consider when choosing a Part D plan is a combination of the plan's premium and how it prices the prescription drugs you take most commonly. The lowest premium may not always produce the lowest-cost plan.

Understanding additional coverage

It should go without saying that even 20 percent of the medical charges not paid by Medicare can be a budget-busting number after a major surgery or extended illness.

This is why you also need to understand the basics of Medicare supplemental coverage. This is an insurance company health care policy that helps cover part or even all of what basic Medicare does not cover. Such coverage is an important safeguard against the potential devastating costs of health care in retirement. There are two ways to subsidize or control the out-of-pocket costs of your health care.

The first is through Medicare Supplements, insurance plans that can be purchased from any number of insurance companies to cover all or part of what Medicare doesn't. These plans offer different options (known in 2017 as plans E through N) that provide a different level of coverage at different premiums. As their name indicates, these plans supplement basic Medicare and pay only after Medicare does. Keep in mind, however, that if you incur charges that Medicare doesn't cover, the supplement plan also will not cover the charges.

Medicare Supplement plans do not utilize a network of medical providers. A supplement plan participant can use any doctor, hospital or other facility that accepts Medicare patients.

None of these supplement plans, however, have prescription drug coverage. A "stand alone" Part D plan must be purchased by people wanting coverage of their pharmaceutical needs.

Another way of limiting out-of-pocket medical costs in retirement involves the use of Medicare Advantage plans, also known as Medicare Part C.

As is the case with Part D drug coverage plans, Medicare has appointed various insurance companies to administer Medicare on its behalf. The insurance companies that offer Advantage plans receive a fixed amount each month from Medicare for the care of its patients.[20] In other words, these plans make payments to medical care providers instead of Medicare. They operate more like standard health care plans in that they have deductibles, co-pays and coinsurance. Medicare's rules for these plans require them to offer the actuarial equivalent of basic Medicare.

There are major advantages to these plans:

• An extremely low premium, or in some cases $0 premium.

---

[20] Medicare.gov. "How do Medicare Advantage Plans Work.?" 2018. https://www.medicare.gov/sign-up-change-plans/types-of-medicare-health-plans/medicare-advantage-plans/how-do-medicare-advantage-plans-work

- A maximum annual out-of-pocket limit.

This limit caps the amount of medical costs an Advantage Plan participant will pay in one year before all other costs are covered at a 100 percent level.

This is important because basic Medicare has no annual out-of-pocket limit, meaning an extremely costly medical procedure could create copays that can quickly drain or even wipe out your retirement savings.

Most Advantage plans include Part D coverage as part of their extremely low or even $0 premium. These plans also offer benefits that basic Medicare does not, such as limited vision, hearing and dental services, as well as membership in exercise plans such as the "Silver Sneakers" program.

Advantage plans are not without their limitations, however. Among them is a cost-control measure that requires plan participants to seek health care from "provider networks" — physicians, hospitals and other providers who have contracted with the insurance companies. Your in-network primary care physician is the "gatekeeper" who usually must provide a referral before you can seek the services of a specialist.

Understanding Medicaid assistance for long-term care

Though Medicare does not cover long-term nursing home care, Medicaid can provide financial assistance to those whose income and assets are low enough to qualify. As noted above, some people look to this source of government assistance as a means of protecting their retirement savings from the expensive ravages of nursing care.

But using Medicaid for nursing home care is not the panacea many people believe it to be.

One, qualifying to receive this aid is complicated and should involve the services of an attorney with a solid background in elder law. Second, Medicaid — though funded by the federal government — is administered by individual states, meaning eligibility rules can vary greatly from state to state and change from year to year. Third, this is not free money; states must try to recoup Medicaid funds spent on nursing care from the estate of the nursing home patient after the death of the patient and any surviving spouse through a process known as Medicaid Recovery.

With all of that in mind, let's take a short tour of what Medicaid eligibility looks like in my home state of Missouri, according to rules in place when this book was being written in 2018.[21]

To be eligible for Medicaid for nursing home care in Missouri, a person must be a Missouri resident age 65 or older and a legal citizen of the United States.

A single person seeking eligibility may own "available resources" — cash, bank accounts, stocks/bonds/securities, homes not being used as a personal residence — with a value of less than $2,000. (The limit is $4,000 for a married couple entering nursing care together.) The person seeking eligibility can own "exempt resources" — assets not included in the formula to determine eligibility — that include the house in which the individual or couple currently resides, one automobile, household goods, burial plots or pre-paid funeral plans, and some life insurance policies with a low face value. An applicant's net monthly income cannot exceed $834 for an individual or $1,129 for a couple.[22] An applicant must also provide a physician's determination that the applicant is in medical need of nursing home care.

---

[21] myDSS. 2018. "MO HealthNet (Medicaid) for Seniors." www.mydss.mo.gov
[22] Persons with monthly incomes in excess of the Missouri state limit can use "spend down" procedures in which medical costs such as prescription drugs, doctor visits, lab costs, dental care and other expenses can be used to reduce monthly income below the limit. For each month you "spend down" your income, Medicaid will pay your medical bills for the remainder of the month. Source: "MO HealthNet (Medicaid) for Seniors." www.mydss.mo.gov

Let's emphasize here that you should not expect Medicaid to pay your entire monthly nursing home expense. Any income available to you — including Social Security — will be applied to the monthly nursing home bill before Medicaid kicks in to help pay the balance. Any state considering your eligibility application will do a five- year "look back" to make sure you didn't just give away assets for the purpose of becoming eligible. Any such activity found in that five-year window can result in a delay of eligibility.

One final thing to consider when deciding whether to pursue Medicaid assistance for nursing home care is the impact of Medicaid Recovery.

This happens after your death and the death of a surviving spouse. This is when your heirs might well receive a bill seeking from your estate the recovery of Medicaid funds spent on your care.

I've seen instances in which adult children of a couple who received Medicaid assistance for nursing care will inherit, say, the $150,000 home of their deceased parents. The house was not a "countable asset" when one or both of their parents applied for Medicaid assistance, but it can be subject to Medicaid Recovery after the death of that parent and any surviving spouse. The kids were more than a little shocked to receive a bill from the state seeking a return of, say, $80,000 in Medicaid assistance spent on the nursing home care of their parent. Technically, this is a lien against the estate of the deceased parents and not against the heirs. But, because the kids inherited the estate, they had to pay the Medicaid Recovery bill, which effectively reduced their total inheritance.

In other words, don't spend all your inheritance until you are absolutely sure all the bills are paid.

All in the family

Outside the realm of health care, family situations also can present roadblocks in retirement. We're talking here about retirees dealing with the problems of their children or grandchildren, or even their own parents, in addition to their own concerns.

Example: I had a retired client with a happy, stable environment in his own home as well as that of his son and family. The son had a good job, so good that his wife retired from teaching to stay home and take care of their kids in a house they'd just purchased.

But then three years later the son lost his job, an $80,000 a year position. One year later, he still can't find work in his chosen field, so he takes a job as a regional manager for a convenience store chain — at less than half his previous salary — basically to provide income and health insurance for his family. His wife had to return to teaching.

The son's family was under obvious stress before his loving parents got involved. My retired client took on his son's house payment for a while, but one day comes to me and says, "I'm tired of making these payments. I'd rather take $92,000 out of my assets right now and pay off his house. I'm tired of watching my son and his family stressed out and struggling. I want to pay off their house. They can repay me whatever they can, when they can, but I want this burden off their backs."

Now, that took a pretty good chunk out of his retirement savings, but it was worth it to him to know his son and his grandkids were not going to be homeless. Not exactly an expenditure he had expected, but one he was in the fortunate position to make.

CHAPTER 6

Building Your Team

A nother huge part of finding the courage to retire comes from having confidence in the people you'll be counting on for advice as you enter this new phase of your life.

To do that, you've got to build a team, much like a general manager of an NFL or Major League Baseball team assembles the players, coaches and staff who give his franchise the best chance to be successful.

This goes well beyond finding the right financial advisor, though this is a significant part of the process.

It likely will take more than one skilled person to address the myriad retirement issues you probably do not yet fully understand. You may, for example, need help with tax matters that are new to retirement. You should finally explore the estate planning you've put off for years. You are likely to deal with matters of insurance coverage — especially when it comes to health care — that are different from anything you've done in your life to this point. You may even find yourself needing banking advice when questions of emergency financing or alternative income arise.

If you know of any one person who can guide you through these issues, please pass along his or her name, as I have yet to meet such a person.

At the same time, it was always my intention in establishing my own business that The Resource Center would become a full-service shop for financial planning services. This does not mean that I alone could handle all the above issues, but I could build a relationship with people who could. That is why I worked to develop a network of professionals with knowledge and experience in insurance, investments, wealth management services, legal matters and banking interests. I sought to help clients build lasting relationships with these professionals who could help guide them through new phases of their lives. I looked for professionals with whom my clients would be comfortable, people they know will be in their corner well in advance of the time they must make critical decisions.

Let's look at some issues that come up often in retirement, as well as how we might go about addressing these concerns.

How will I know that the assets I leave behind — the things I spent my entire life amassing — are left to the people I want to have them? What is involved in the process of estate planning? Must I have a will to make this determination, or can I get by on pay-on-death instructions, joint tenancy agreements or beneficiary designations? Do I need to go a step beyond making a will and establish a trust? What are the pros and cons of the two? And most important, who do I see about all of this?

Here is where an attorney should be part of your team. Preferably someone with a background in estate planning and elder law as opposed to a lawyer who does a bit of everything. We'll address this in considerably more detail later in this chapter.

I keep hearing about a potential "tax bomb" when required minimum distributions kick in at age 70½. I've heard something about "provisional income" and how it determines whether I owe tax on my Social Security benefits, but I don't fully understand how this works. I'm told I should consider moving tax-deferred money from my IRA accounts into a more tax-advantageous Roth IRA where this money will never be taxed again. I understand that I must pay tax immediately on any such Roth conversion money, but how and when is the best way to do this in the most tax advantageous way possible?

Here is where an accountant or tax attorney can be a helpful part of your team. For, while your financial advisor can give you the reasoning and means for moving IRA money into Roth accounts, it may take an accountant to dig into your personal numbers and formulate a plan on the most tax-efficient way to do so.

I understand the basics of Medicare, which means I also know that Medicare doesn't cover everything. But there's still so much I don't know. What is Medigap coverage? What is Medicare Advantage? What is the Part D "donut hole?" To whom do I turn for answers to these questions?

Here is where an insurance specialist should be part of your team. Someone who can explain in as much detail as you need the complicated parts of your health care coverage in retirement, specifically how Medicare Supplement or Medicare Advantage coverage can help you cover the costs that Medicare doesn't. Someone to help you understand deductibles, coinsurance, copays and out-of-pocket costs.

How does one go about meeting all these professionals?

Often, these are relationships you may have established on your own over the years. The more typical process, however, involves making these contacts through a financial advisor who is likely to be one of the first members of your team. This will be someone most likely to alert you to the need for professionals, and someone with a network he or she can confidently refer to clients.

Keep in mind, too, that building your team is a process you would ideally start five to 10 years before retirement, though it rarely is ever too late to add a professional to your support team.

The role of the financial advisor

I will always admire people with foresight who first become associated with a financial advisor well before retirement age. These are people with an eye on their future who often seek help in making investment decisions in their 30s or early 40s.

I always hope these advisors help their clients make sound investing choices based on a risk/reward level that is in the client's best interest at any particular part of their life. I further hope this client/advisor relationship involves trust and holds up to the test of time.

At the same time, however, I also know some advisors who skillfully help clients build a retirement nest egg may not be the best guides when it comes time to convert those savings into lifelong income. The worlds of accumulation and distribution can be very different. Consequently, a person entering or preparing to enter retirement must be confident that an advisor they may have worked with for years is as knowledgeable about turning assets into income as they were about amassing wealth.

Part of finding the confidence to retire involves securing a financial advisor who understands the importance of sustainable lifetime income; the implications of when to begin taking Social Security benefits; the basics of Medicare and supplemental health-care coverage; the challenge of funding long-term care such as nursing home costs; the importance of estate and legacy planning.

The advisor with whom you've worked closely in your accumulation years may be the person to take you into the income/distribution phase. But if you have any doubts — if you suspect your advisor is more interested in pushing investment products (however good they might be) than in securing lifelong income for yourself — then it may be in your interest to make an advisor experienced in retirement income strategies a member of your team.

This is someone who will guide you through a completely new phase of your life. Someone who understands the unique challenges that arise when you are no longer working and drawing a weekly paycheck, someone to help you enter the scary new world of "fixed income."

Someone who understands the financial drain that comes with medical expenses that rise as our age does, and who has options to deal with those concerns.

Someone who understands both the emotional, physical and financial stress of dealing with elderly parents, or the desire to help adult children.

Someone who understands the fear of outliving one's money is more than just a financial industry catchphrase.

I believe the financial advisor who will guide you into and through retirement must have experience in dealing with the special needs of this new period in life. This person should be familiar not only with IRA rollovers and provisional income and Medigap coverage, but also a person who can steer you to professionals in elder law and legacy planning, tax planning strategies and options for funding long-term care such as nursing home costs.

It must be someone willing to say, "If I can't help you with such issues, I certainly know and trust someone who will."

My theory has long been that most people first start thinking about these issues only after being prodded initially by their financial advisor. This is when they first consider adding other qualified professionals to their team.

These new team members will understand more than just the conventional wisdom about what works well for most people. They must above all else consider what might work best for you. That means each member must understand your financial goals, your objectives and priorities. Such knowledge often comes from working closely with your advisor.

This is all part of building a team, one that most likely has your advisor as its general manager.

The role of the attorney

It's a comment I hear most frequently when first talking about estate planning with a client or a married couple.

Why do we need estate planning, many people will ask, when we don't have enough to constitute what most people would call an estate?

Well, let's make something clear here at the start.

One, you don't need to live in a mansion to have an estate. Whether you know it or not, you have one now, even though your name isn't Bill Gates. If you own a home, a bank account, stocks/bonds/CDs, a car, a boat, any collectables, life insurance, personal property — anything of value — then you have an estate. Estate planning is the process of establishing the most efficient way to distribute these assets, no matter how big or small, after your death.

You might not realize this, either, but just as you have an estate, you also have an estate plan in place. Not that it's an especially good plan.

The state in which you reside has developed it, and it's called "probate." A probate court must legally decide how to distribute any assets you leave behind should you die "intestate," which means dying without a will. A probate court also will decide who will handle your affairs while you are living — that is, appoint a "conservator" if you have not already done so — should you become incapacitated and unable to make decisions. It also will appoint a custodian, who may or may not be your first choice for the responsibility, should minor children suddenly lose parents who failed to make this designation in a will.

A will is one way

A will is a bare minimum estate planning document, but for some people it will suffice when it comes to establishing their intentions regarding the distribution of property and assets after their death.

A properly designed will names an executor who not only oversees the distribution of your assets according to your instructions, but who also will settle any payment of taxes and debts that must be resolved before your assets can be dispersed. A will written by anyone with minor children should also include a provision naming one or more guardians.

A quick explanation may be necessary here to explain the difference between "executor" and "power of attorney," as many people confuse the two responsibilities. An executor acts as the will maker's representative after death; power of attorney applies only when the will maker is alive. In giving a trusted family member or friend your power of attorney, you empower this person to make decisions on your behalf should you become incapacitated and unable to do so yourself. The power of attorney disappears at the time of your death, at which time the decision-making passes to the executor. The two roles are different, meaning that a person wanting to do estate planning via a will is well advised to also consider a power of attorney designation as part of the process.

Your executor is your representative, typically with the help of an attorney, throughout the probating of your estate. This can be a costly and time-consuming process. Some states assess probate administrative costs ranging from 3 to 8 percent of the total estate being settled, and some probate cases can take six months to a year or more to complete. The distribution of assets to your intended heirs is frozen until the process is completed.

A will by itself has other limitations, as well.

One, a will must be validated or approved by a probate court before assets can be distributed. Second, all matters in probate court are public record, meaning anyone can learn that your will is before the court and can access that will. Moreover, anyone can contest a will. It might be a family member, but anyone with a claim against your estate — someone trying to collect an unpaid bill, for instance — can stake their claim in probate court. Some of these claims are legitimate; others, sadly, may not be. Beyond that, anyone with claims against your heirs can make claims against the estate that will ultimately benefit those heirs.

Moreover, a will often does not accomplish the basic things the will maker set out to do. It is merely a directive — "Give this stuff to this person" — but it establishes no means by which this is done. This is why a probate court becomes involved.

On the positive side, not all estate assets are subject to probate. Jointly owned assets can pass directly to a surviving spouse without probate, as can assets such as life insurance, annuities and IRA accounts that have designated beneficiaries.

Even with all these limitations, however, it should go without saying that drawing up a will is preferable to doing nothing at all and having a probate court make all decisions about your estate in your absence.

In trusts we trust

If a will represents the bare minimum, a trust is the gold standard.

A revocable living trust — a legal document that can be changed or eliminated completely while you are still alive — effectively establishes a kind of secured vault into which all elements of your estate are kept and protected. The contents of the vault are put there by you, the trust maker (or grantor) at the time you "fund" the trust — that is, title your assets to the trust.

Distributions of the vault's contests are overseen by a trustee designated by the trust maker(s). This person, persons or institution have a legal obligation to follow the instructions you leave as part of the trust documents. While you are living, you and/or a spouse are the first trustees of everything in the "vault; you can access your assets just as you always did. Upon the passing of one partner, the survivor becomes the sole trustee. Upon that person's death, a successor trustee designated by the grantors oversees the trust and makes any distributions from it. This trustee can be a family member or members, a trusted friend or an institution such as a bank's trust department.

Elements of a revocable living trust typically include a:

• Pour-over will, a document in which you declare that all assets not previously titled to the trust to be so designated.

• Durable power of attorney giving your designated representative the power to make financial decisions on your behalf should you become incapacitated and unable to make your intentions known. As noted above, the power of attorney exists only while you are alive.

• Separate power of attorney for health matters. This is a person empowered to make important medical decisions for you should you be unable to do so yourself.

• Living will/medical directive that spells out your medical care choices (such as whether extreme life-saving measures shall be applied in end-of-life situations).

• HIPAA declaration designating which family members or people important to you can receive your medical information from a health care provider.

Real estate deeds, asset assignment instructions and any other pertinent instructions involving the distribution of personal property such as family heirlooms.

A major advantage of a trust over a will is that a trust avoids the time-consuming, costly and public probate process. A properly funded trust — that is, one with all estate assets correctly "titled" into the trust — can speed the distribution of these assets to the people you want to have them. The holdings of the trust are not subject to claims by creditors. A trust can designate how and when your assets will be distributed. This can be helpful if you want assets going to minor children not yet ready to handle large sums, or to heirs involved in divorce or perhaps substance abuse.

Let's acknowledge here that the cost of establishing a trust is generally higher than the price an attorney is likely to charge for drawing up a will. In my Springfield, Missouri, business, I try to refer clients to estate attorneys I know and trust who typically charge between $1,500 and $4,000 to establish an estate plan.

Now for the big question: How do you know whether your estate interests can be adequately handled by a will, or if you need to go to the added expense of establishing a trust?

This is a daunting issue for anyone who's never talked about estate planning, and this is where you want both a trusted financial advisor and an estate attorney as part of your team.

It helps to educate yourself on at least some basics of estate planning before you retain an attorney. A financial advisor with the proper background should be able to walk you through the basics of non-probate transfers such as pay-on-death bank accounts; transfer-on-death documents involving personal property such as cars and boats; beneficiary and contingent beneficiary designations on your retirement and investment accounts; a beneficiary deed on your house as well as the bare-bones structure of probate, living wills, powers of attorney and other legal topics.

But a financial advisor must also know his limitations when it comes to dealing with legal issues. I certainly know mine.

People go to law school for at least three years to learn about these complex legal matters, and some attorneys even restrict their practice to elder law. I'm not an attorney — though I work closely with several on behalf of clients — so I'm not going to even attempt a law school review of estate planning here. But, we can talk in general about some basics, including some common situations faced by people trying to decide between drawing up a will or a trust.

Some hypothetical examples

Example 1:

Let's look first at the example of a widow. Let's say for the purpose of this illustration that she's 70, that she rents her house and has maybe $50,000 to $60,000 in annuities. She's got another $25,000 to $30,000 in cash in her bank accounts and CDs. She doesn't own a car because her daughter lives with her and helps her get around. She's got some possessions that represent all her personal property, but they don't amount to much.

We began the process of estate planning for this woman by noting that her assets and needs are relatively simple.

She wants her daughter to receive the cash in her bank accounts at the time of her death, and she can accomplish this by establishing a pay-on-death arrangement with her bank.

Note here, however, that Mom **does not** want to establish co-ownership of her bank accounts with her daughter while she is still alive. Doing so could result in someone to whom her daughter owes money — say, in an injury-related lawsuit — gaining access to Mom's money. Mom could instead provide emergency access to those bank accounts by giving her daughter durable power of attorney, an arrangement that gives her daughter the power to write checks from Mom's account should Mom become physically or mentally unable to do so herself.

Mom would normally also need a transfer-on-death arrangement on any vehicles she owns, though that's not necessary here as she doesn't own any. If she owned a house, which she didn't, she also would want to establish a beneficiary deed on the home, most likely in her daughter's name. She also must be sure she has named beneficiaries on her annuities so that any cash value remaining in the contracts will go to whoever she wants at the time of her death without being exposed to probate.

This woman has friends telling her she needed a trust. She, however, believed her assets could be adequately distributed through a less expensive will. Consulting with an attorney might give her the following options.

Yes, at the very least she needed a will that named an executor and provided instructions for distributing her assets and personal property. She also needed to establish a durable power of attorney for financial decisions, as well as a separate power of attorney for health care decisions. She might also consider drawing up a living will/medical directive that stated her intentions regarding end-of-life medical treatment. She might also consider drawing up a HIPAA declaration determining to whom her health care providers could release information about her medical condition.

She is, in short, looking at many of the components routinely included in a basic revocable trust. The costs of drawing up some or all of the above legal documents, quite frankly, may be only slightly less than the expenses involved in establishing a trust. The decision of whether to take the extra step at an extra expense is entirely up to her.

Here is another factor that might affect her decision. The non-probate transfers described above — the pay-on-death and transfer-on-death designations, as well as the beneficiary deed on a home — can encounter problems. This is especially true when a beneficiary of such a transfer dies before or at the same time as the will maker or is otherwise in no position to receive money from a bank account or transfer of property. These non-probate transfers typically make no contingency designations, a potential problem that can be addressed in a trust.

For the record, I'm not suggesting here that everyone absolutely *must* have a trust. The woman described above, for example, might well have her assets distributed according to her instructions through a will, along with some pay-on-death arrangements and a power of attorney designation.

I would suggest, however, that most readers of this book have assets that are more involved than those of the woman described above. Very seldom have I encountered a client who would not have benefited from having a fully developed trust. This is especially true both from a privacy and a simplicity standpoint.

In my opinion — and keep in mind that I am not an attorney — a trust just makes things so much easier for heirs at a time when they are dealing with the painful loss of a loved one. From my experience, using a will alone to settle an estate often requires heirs to jump through costly probate hoops in a public setting over an extended time frame. With a trust, however, they usually can get estate matters resolved relatively quickly, privately and efficiently.

Remember, the motto of my company is "Simple solutions in a complex world." And though a will might seem less complex in structure than a trust, carrying out its directives can be far more difficult than you might imagine.

In my experience, developing a trust that avoids the time, expense and public nature of probate court, and which provides a vault of assets that can be opened and distributed relatively quickly and according to your instructions, is a more simple and efficient way of distributing your assets when you are no longer here.

Example 2:

Let's look now at a hypothetical couple whose estate assets are considerably more complicated than those of the lady in Example 1.

This client couple owned a farm of about 120 acres with a house, a barn and other farm equipment. The total value was approximately $400,000. They also had about $300,000 in investments with me in both qualified and nonqualified IRA accounts. They had another $100,000 in money market accounts and CDs. They owned two cars as well as a motorized bass boat with a trailer. The rest of their personal property included a few collectables. Add it up and they were looking at maybe $900,000 in hard assets, cash and land.

They had two kids who got along well and would split the estate 50-50 when Mom and Dad both passed.

There were a couple different ways we could go here in beginning estate planning for this couple.

With just the two kids willing to split everything 50-50, this couple might consider "getting by" with pay-on-death arrangements on their bank accounts; a transfer-on-death arrangement on the cars and the boat; a beneficiary deed that gave the farm house and land to the two children after the passing of both parents; contingent beneficiary designations on the IRA accounts, again dividing all assets 50-50; legal documents establishing power of attorney for both financial matters and health care issues; a medical directive regarding end-of-life medical treatment; and the drafting of a will that establishes an executor who will oversee the probate process and handle all distributions from the estate according to instructions included in the will.

You guessed it. We're once again talking about most of the components of a typical revocable living trust.

But let's complicate things even further.

Let's now say that grandkids also are involved, and now our farm couple wants to leave something for all six of them, say $10,000 each. Let's also hypothesize that the son wants the farm while the daughter doesn't. Let's further suppose that, in an attempt to divide the estate equally, the son says he'll take the farm and equipment worth around $400,000, while the sister will take the IRA accounts worth around $300,000. The son agrees to make things fair for his sister by paying her $50,000 — half of the $100,000 difference between what he will get for the farm and what she will receive for the IRA accounts. Both hope to end up with around $350,000 each from the distribution of the farm property and the IRA investments.

We also have to account for the couple's desire to pass something along to the six grandkids — two of whom are the son's children and four of them the daughter's children.

How do you accomplish all those things?

Here is where a properly funded trust — meaning one with all the couple's assets properly titled to the trust, along with detailed instructions regarding the distribution of those assets, can make the transfer of an estate easier for all concerned.

Frankly, addressing all of these multiple intentions would be extremely difficult to accomplish with only a simple will that could be challenged by any of the interested parties. That might be either of the two children — especially if one claimed the other broke a promise about making equal distribution — or any one of the six grandchildren. Or, it could be challenged by anyone else who might stake a claim against the couple's estate upon learning from public records that the estate is subject to probate.

A trust, however, moves the prospect of probate court out of the equation.

A trust that holds all assets of the farm couple's estate should spell out in advance how all these assets will be distributed according to the couple's designation. The farm to the son; the IRA accounts to the daughter; a "make-even payment" from the son to his sister; the specific distribution of the bank accounts' cash to the grandkids. The successor trustee — the person, persons or institution designated as trustee following the deaths of both parents — will decide when to make the $10,000 payments to, say, a minor grandchild not yet ready to handle a large sum of money. That trustee might also decide whether to limit or even temporarily withhold a distribution to a grandchild deemed incapable of handling such a gift because of, say, substance abuse or domestic problems.

This would be a situation where you would want an estate attorney as part of your team in an attempt to head off problems that may arise after you leave us in advance of your departure.

When, and how, should I begin estate planning?

For people with minor children, sooner is better. You want some kind of determination made for their care in your unexpected absence, as well as providing for them financially should you and your spouse be tragically taken at the same time. Without any such designation in a will or trust, a court will appoint a guardian and will control the access of the children to their inheritance until the time they turn 18.

Typically, however, most people don't start thinking about estate planning until much later in life when they start hearing friendly reminders about legacy planning from older family members or financial advisors.

Unfortunately for some, they run out of the time they'd always assumed they would have to "get around to it someday soon."

Why are most people so reluctant to begin estate planning?

I've found over the years that many people put it off because they don't know where to start, they don't know who to talk to, or they are deterred by the cost. Dealing with the inevitability of one's own mortality also is a factor.

What are some of the toughest aspects of estate planning?

Surprisingly, determining the components of your estate isn't especially difficult. A visit with your financial advisor prior to your first meeting with an estate attorney can address many of these issues. A sit-down session at the dinner table can often address most issues of valued personal property.

In doing all this, you may find you've done much of this planning already. If you've already designated contingent beneficiaries on your investment accounts and life insurance policies, you're well on your way. Deciding who wants what among family heirlooms or personal keepsakes might take a few phone calls to decide. Even then, keep in mind that decisions you make now aren't necessarily written in stone. You can always change components of a will or revocable trust, provided you have the mental or physical capacity to do so.

The cost of estate planning? It's very likely less expensive today than when your parents did it. As I mentioned earlier, the estate plans I help clients establish usually cost somewhere between $1,500 and $4,000.

One of the most unique parts of estate planning might be educating the attorney about you, the new client for whom he or she will prepare a will or trust.

This is because no cookie-cutter approach can fit each individual or couple. Your attorney can't make a recommendation on what might work best for your needs until he fully understands your assets, your desires, your goals, your family dynamic. Your close-knit family of four may be vastly different than the four-person household just down the street that has a daughter going through a divorce or a son in rehabilitation. That family may not be as anxious as you are to do an equal division of assets between children.

Keep in mind, too, that having a trust document alone is not the ultimate solution to problems that might arise in the distribution of your assets after your death. I've seen far too many trusts that don't accomplish what the trust maker intended because they weren't properly funded — that is, the assets intended for distribution were never properly "titled" within the trust. This process is not complicated but it does require some attention to detail.

One other note here. In working with a client's estate attorney in establishing a trust, I often try to determine who will do what in the process of funding the trust. Who, for instance, will go to the county office for the beneficiary deed on the home? Who will go to the licensing bureau to secure transfer-on-death on a car? Who goes to the bank to establish pay-on-death provisions on bank accounts, as well as making the trust — again, which you control while you are living — the legal owner of all accounts.

In most cases, a client can avoid additional fees and charges by doing this legwork on their own. Even then, I try to provide clients with written instructions of the specific requests to be made on a visit to a county assessor, or a bank or the local DMV. It's part of the full-service nature I so strongly believe in.

Bottom line, estate planning is a complex issue in which you need competent people to help you navigate the process. In establishing a trust, you need to work closely with your financial advisor, your attorney, your bank and your insurance agent to make sure that all essential accounts are properly sheltered by the trust.

I know, there are many online services available who claim you can do you own legal work — at a considerably reduced cost — in drawing up your own will. Some services even offer documents to establish a trust. While I firmly believe in simple solutions in a complex world, estate planning usually involves seeking specialized help to assure the orderly transfer of your lifelong assets when you are no longer here to oversee the process.

Beyond that, it is equally important to make sure your trust is updated frequently. Life throws frequent changes at us that might include the death of a beneficiary or successor trustee. There might be changes in a family situation involving divorce, a legal complication or a medical matter. You may have added new property, new vehicles, new investment accounts since establishing the trust. A trust should be reviewed at least every couple of years to ensure that everything is up to date. Having a team member looking out for your best interests is a good way to make sure this happens.

The role of the accountant or tax professional

I would not suggest here that everyone needs a certified public accountant, though a CPA can be invaluable if your financial affairs involve a business or are otherwise complex. But, having access to at least a tax professional can be important, especially in the early years of dealing with tax issues that are unique to retirement.

We're talking here about dealing with matters such as required minimum distributions and the effect they and other types of retirement income can have on provisional income, the number that determines how much (if any) of your Social Security income is subject to tax.

A tax professional also can be worth his or her fee in helping with matters of Roth conversions — the process of moving tax-deferred money from qualified accounts such as IRAs into more tax- favorable Roth IRA accounts. An accountant or tax professional can help you evaluate your tax situation in the years before you must begin taking RMDs (at age 70½) from tax-deferred IRAs. This tax specialist can advise you on the most tax opportune time to move money into a Roth IRA by showing you the tax effect of different amounts you might be considering for transfer. Remember, you will pay tax now on any money involved in a Roth conversion, but you will never pay tax again on funds once they are within a Roth. A tax specialist can help you determine that best time to make such a conversion.

Keep in mind here that a tax professional need not be a licensed CPA or tax attorney. A tax preparer with whom you have a relationship over the years might also be helpful. A tax preparer at a national tax firm or at a local or regional office can be worth their fee to guide you through retirement-related tax filing issues that may be new to you.

Again, the key here — as is the case with assembling all members of your tax team — is finding someone you trust and feel comfortable with.

The role of the insurance agent

It should not surprise anyone who has read this far into this book to know that I am a big believer in independent insurance agencies, such as mine at The Resource Center.

Let's note the difference here between an independent agent and one commonly known as the captive agent — one employed by a national company whose main efforts will be in selling the insurance products of that parent company. An independent agent, however, is not tied to the products of any one or two companies but has access to policies from a wide variety of companies that give you more choices to help address your specific needs.

The bottom line here is how each insurance agent or company responds to your needs when you need them most. If you're vacationing, for example, and some calamity befalls your car, your boat, your camper or yourself, a captive agent can easily put you in contact with a local agent of his company. But, the same can be said of your local independent agent, who also can put you in contact with an agent in the vicinity of the incident for which you need help. The claims adjuster would handle that situation, they could assign someone locally to help you with your claim.

Here is the area in which I really believe in the value of a relationship you've developed over time with a local representative.

Let's say the company currently writing the insurance on your home decides it has to raise premiums to cover the numerous claims they are paying because of natural disasters elsewhere in the country. When you're on a fixed income in retirement, you're not in a position to routinely accommodate such increases.

The "captive" agent trying to keep your premiums level after such a company-mandated increase may raise your deductible or decrease your coverage. But an independent agent with whom you have a relationship can go shopping among many different insurance companies in search of a policy that could put your coverage, cost and deductibles more in range with what you had previously. The flexibility of the independent agent — especially one with whom you have a long relationship and who is working with your interest in mind — can be very valuable at a time of rising premiums.

Let's now turn briefly to the idea of using different types of insurance coverage in retirement.

As we mentioned earlier, this is a time of life when you might look at life insurance as a way of addressing needs that are different from those you covered earlier in life. Now is the time when you might be looking at long-term care insurance. Or, an agent with whom you have a relationship might help devise a way of leveraging RMD money into life insurance policies that not only create a tax-free death benefit for your heirs, but also features riders allowing you to use part of that death benefit to assist with long-term care while you are still living.

Now also is the time when you will want to explore supplemental health care insurance that covers the medical expenses Medicare does not. Such policies are sold by many different companies — your mailbox is undoubtedly overflowing with offers every fall around renewal time. But, by establishing a relationship with a specialist in Medicare supplemental coverage — and we have just such a person available at The Resource Center — you can inform yourself to the point that you acquire the confidence to know whatever supplemental insurance or Medicare Advantage plan you choose is the best for your needs at any stage of your life.

The role of the banker

Most towns in America have one or more community banks or are close to one in a neighboring town. I'm a big believer in these community banks — and not just because I have an ownership interest in one here in Missouri — and the level of individualized service they can provide to their local clients.

What is the main reason most people give for keeping accounts in a major national bank?

Well, they are convenient with branch offices throughout the country. If I'm visiting in Florida or vacationing in Arizona, the chances are I will find a branch of my national bank somewhere in the area. I'll be able to use my ATM card without fees at many different places throughout the nation. I'll have access to a banker should some special need arise away from home.

But today we live in such a modern age that even your local banker is never far away.

Customers of the community bank in which I have an interest quickly find we are part of networks that offer access to ATM machines all over the country. They also find they can easily access a representative of their hometown bank from anywhere in the country.

Say you're travelling and some emergency happens for which you need money immediately transferred into your checking account. Most people can easily access their accounts online and make a transfer of funds. Or, for those who do not do online banking, a telephone call to a community banker with whom you have a relationship can produce the transfer of funds you are seeking.

Your community banker also can be an important resource should you encounter special income needs that often arise in retirement.

The bottom line: Your financial goals, objectives, priorities

In ending this discussion of team building and the development of professional relationships, let's make a final point about the importance of each team member understanding your financial goals, objectives and priorities. That will not happen unless you establish a working relationship with each.

Your estate planner must understand your legacy goals as well as the needs of the people you want to provide for when you are no longer here. Your independent insurance agent needs to understand your financial situation so that in the event of, say, a homeowners' insurance rate hike, he or she knows to start looking for a new policy. Your estate attorney should understand that you want practical legal advice that is affordable and fits your needs. Specifically, if your estate planning is relatively simple and can be handled with a will and power of attorney documents and beneficiary designations, then don't try to sell me a trust.

People often don't know what they need, or even what to ask for in retirement. Yet there are lots of attorneys, financial advisors, tax attorneys, insurance agents or professionals and others who are more interested in doing things that benefit their bottom line more than yours. It often can be hard to figure out the right thing to do. This is where trust comes in, as well as education. Knowing you have relationships with professionals that have your goals, objectives and priorities in mind is important. So is educating yourself on the things you need so that you can articulate your desires to the specialists on your team and be in better position to help them help you.

CHAPTER 7

Annuities: Stop This Crazy Ride, I Want to Get Off

D o you remember the Great Recession, that time of economic turmoil from late 2007 through the spring of 2009?

Yeah, I know; silly question. I'd like to forget it too, but time has eased only some of the painful memories of that period. Time also has allowed many people to recover nicely — some to even flourish — in the decade since then.

Even so, time can't completely wipe out the memory of many investors who watched in horror back then as their investment portfolio lost 30 to 40 percent or more in value. Granted, many investors who avoided much of the panic selling of that period likely recovered, eventually, what they lost in account value during the market recovery that began in 2009 and continued for the next several years. But not everyone felt comfortable "holding the line" while waiting for the recovery.

Among the members of that latter group were people in or nearing retirement who wondered if they would have the time necessary to see their retirement nest eggs recoup what had been lost to plummeting market conditions.

As I've indicated elsewhere in this book, my company deals with many clients who are in or near retirement. And while I don't purport to speak for them all, I can characterize a common refrain heard from many of them during and immediately after the Great Recession. To wit:

"Wow, that was one wild, crazy ride. I'm not sure I have the stomach to go on that one again."

Well, here's some news that will hardly qualify as "breaking."

Folks, there will be more economic downturns and recessions in our future; while no one can predict what will happen in the future, history shows us they have happened every 10 years or so. To be sure, I believe most are not likely to be as severe or financially painful as the one throughout all of 2008, but any downturn has the potential to be painful for retirees depending on market-based assets to produce their income.

There is, sadly, no ironclad protection against the effects of a recession. One could take all of one's financial assets, convert them to cash, lock that money in a vault for a year and still find the earning power of that cash reduced slightly by the effect of inflation alone. Even a conservatively managed portfolio with a large blend of bonds and low-volatility securities offers no guarantee against loss, especially in times of inflation and rising interest rates.

So, what is a retiree or a person nearing retirement to do to gain some degree of protection for the retirement nest egg one will depend on for the rest of their life?

Allow me to suggest that one way to at least smooth out the bumps of a rocky recession road is through the use of insurance products that offer protection against loss of principal due to market volatility as well as a contractual guarantee of income based on the claims-paying ability of the insurance company issuing the contract.

As you've no doubt guessed by now — based on sentiments I've expressed often throughout this book — I'm talking here about annuity products that function in a variety of ways to offer protection of principal in times of market volatility, interest-created growth and future income during the payout phase of a contract.

The basics of annuities

To understand why I'm such a big fan of some annuity products — including my own personal preference for the fixed index annuity — and why I believe the stability they provide merits a place somewhere in the portfolio of many of my retirement-age clients, let's first explore some annuity basics.

By definition, an annuity is an insurance contract designed primarily to provide income. The insurance company writing the contract accepts money from the contract owner in the form of premium payments. The company in turn promises to make regular income payments over an extended period to an annuitant who can be either the contract holder or anyone else designated as a beneficiary. That payout period can cover the remaining lifetime of the annuitant or even a spouse if the contract so designates.

The insurance company's promise to make regular income payments is backed by the claims-paying ability of the company. Each company's solvency — that is, its ability to meet all its long-term financial obligations — is overseen by regulatory agencies in each state in which a company operates. Most states require an insurance company to maintain financial reserves of at least one dollar for every dollar the company receives in premiums.

Investors concerned about the safety of money held by an insurance company can also access solvency ratings computed by independent rating services such as Standard and Poor, A.M. Best, Fitch, and Moody's.

I mention these safeguards only because people with reservations about annuity purchases sometimes express concern about the relative safety of their money. And yes, when planning an annuity purchase, you need to make sure you are working with a reliable, top-rated insurance company.

At the same time, however, I believe many of these concerns to be overstated given the track record of today's insurance companies, as well as the oversights described above. Historically, most insurance companies have survived even the most difficult of financial times, something that can't be said for many banks and other financial lending institutions.

Can I get my money out of an annuity?

Other people with concerns about annuities worry about their ability to access the money they've invested, so let's spend a quick minute discussing that.

True, an annuity contract should be considered a long-term prospect. This isn't a bank account where you deposit and withdraw funds as you need. Annuities are not a "day trading" operation where you can buy a stock, wait a few days or weeks for a price hike, then sell your shares and take your profit. An annuity is not even as liquid as a holding in a typical brokerage account.

Rather, it is a long-term commitment by the insurance company to hold and grow your principal until such time as you elect to begin receiving regular income payments. These payments made on a monthly, quarterly or annual basis will occur over a designated period that can — depending on the contract — last for as long as you or your spouse live.

The income payments typically begin after several years of an annuity's "accumulation phase." During this growth period, many contracts feature a "surrender period," during which you pay a penalty for withdrawing part or all of your invested premium.

There are exceptions to the above rule. One involves the "immediate annuity," an insurance contract that has no accumulation period. (We'll address the immediate annuity elsewhere in this chapter.) Other annuity contracts allow a contract holder in the surrender period to withdraw a small percentage of principal — typically no more than 10 percent — without incurring a surrender charge. Many contracts also allow a contract owner access to principal in the event of nursing home confinement, diagnosis of a terminal illness or unemployment. Sometimes this exception to the application of surrender charges is available through an optional rider, sometimes it is part of the base contract provisions.

Surrender periods vary greatly from contract to contract. Some last only a couple of years; others last up to 10 years or more. As time passes and the surrender period shortens, so does the penalty for early withdrawal. When the surrender period ends, you are free to take penalty-free income as you need, or even withdraw your principal and all growth in the account in a lump sum. Or, you can always opt for a system of regular payouts.

Tax-related early withdrawal concerns

The tax-advantageous nature of annuities also creates a limitation on early withdrawals.

Because principal in an annuity is allowed to grow on a tax-deferred basis, taking distributions before a contract owner reaches age 59½ is strongly discouraged by the IRS. The government will, in fact, assess a 10 percent tax as a penalty on any amount withdrawn before that time. Moreover, any amount withdrawn also is taxed as ordinary income, meaning you incur the ordinary income tax rate and the additional 10 percent penalty.

But let's not paint a completely negative picture here by overlooking the tax advantages of an annuity.

Annuity payments made with pre-tax dollars — as part of a "qualified" retirement plan — do not count against that year's taxable income. This happens because the IRS considers annuities part of a retirement program.

Keep in mind, however, that you must pay tax on this money someday. Income taken from qualified annuities — both the invested principal and any growth from interest in the account — is fully taxable at the time of distribution.

Also note that purchasing an annuity inside a qualified plan (such as a retirement plan) that provides a tax deferral under the Internal Revenue Code provides no additional tax benefits. An annuity used to fund a tax-qualified retirement plan should be selected based on features other than the tax deferral. All of the annuity's features, risks, limitations and costs should be considered prior to purchasing an annuity inside a qualified retirement plan. An annuity funded by after-tax dollars — a "nonqualified" annuity — gives you no advantage in the tax year you pay the premium. But, when you take income from this account, only the interest in the account is taxed. The money you paid in premiums is not taxed again.

Let's further note that any tax-deferred growth in an annuity does not factor in the "provisional income" formula that determines how much, if any, of your Social Security benefits are subject to taxation. Income from investment dividends such as those from stocks and bonds, as well as regular interest from CDs, are part of that formula.

Let's also note that investments in nonqualified annuities are not subject to the annual limits placed on investments to an IRA, 401(k) or Roth IRA. Nonqualified annuities and Roth IRAs also are not subject to required minimum distributions at age 70½.

But what about the high annuity fees I hear so much about?

Sure, the fee structure of an annuity is something you need to discuss in detail with your advisor as part of making an informed decision about whether this financial tool is right for you.

There are a number of different types of annuities, and the costs and fees vary widely. Often, the cost for the product is built into its pricing, and is reflected in its guarantees, payout rates and other factors. It isn't always easy to know exactly what an annuity "costs," so we often recommend that our clients also evaluate the true value the annuity's guaranteed income can provide in addition to their actual "costs."

Smooth out the potentially bumpy ride

Allow me to wrap up this introductory section on annuities by acknowledging that I've addressed some negative perceptions regarding them here at the outset. My reason for doing so is because I often have to dispel such concerns before I can make a client appreciate the positives that can come with annuities.

Bottom line here: No market-based investment can guarantee a stream of income like an annuity can. Furthermore, no investment can guarantee you a steady source of money that you cannot outlive as an annuity can. Finally, few investment products can offer the financial hedge against risk and protection from losses due to market fluctuations that an annuity can. Today's fixed index annuity is a financial tool that guarantees income, protects against loss of principal, provides the potential for market index-based interest credits. The fixed index annuity, however, will not give you market-like returns. Interest you can earn, while based on the movement of an external market index, is limited by caps, spreads and participation rates.

Principal protection, income, growth potential. These are qualities you need in at least part of your retirement savings and income plan. I would go as far as to suggest it should occupy a large part.

Now, don't misunderstand me here. I wouldn't suggest for a minute that there is no room in a retirement portfolio for at least some element of risk taken in the hope of realizing a greater reward. It is entirely up to you to decide what level of the risk-reward curve you are comfortable riding in retirement. Some people are very comfortable taking that ride. More power to them.

But, for others who think it's time to get off the ride before they fall off, I gladly suggest they consider if an annuity may be a suitable alternative as a way to smooth out a potentially bumpy ride.

I am not advocating, mind you, that annuities are for everyone. But some kind of annuity may be part of your life whether you know it or not.

That company or government pension plan you may be part of? It functions similar to an annuity in some regard. The company or government agency made payments into a retirement fund on behalf of its employees. In theory, that pool of money is invested and expanded. Retired employees receive regular pension payments from the fund for however long the recipient designates.

Well, that's the way things are supposed to work — and the way they worked successfully in the past — with defined-benefit pension plans.

Today, sadly, these defined-benefit plans are not as common as they once were after being replaced by 401(k) plans funded primarily through employee contributions with some match by the employer. Worse yet, many private pension plans in recent years went underfunded or were raided by the corporation or government agency maintaining them, leading to broken promises and extremely anxious pensioners who no longer were receiving the retirement income they were promised.

The demise of defined benefit pension plans, along with the market volatility to which most 401(k)s are exposed, are among the reasons I encourage my clients to consider the role of the fixed index annuity in their retirement planning, where it makes sense for them. Again, this is a contract that promises a steady flow of regular income — income that can last for the lifetimes of two spouses, if desired — while protecting against loss of principal even as it provides the potential for interest credits.

Principal protection, income, growth potential. This is an example of what I mean by "simple solutions in a complex world."

The family of annuities

An annuity can have different forms and options for both growing the contract value (during the accumulation phase) as well as providing income (during the distribution or "payout" phase). The type of annuity you might choose depends entirely on your objectives, priorities and goals, but the bottom line on any annuity is its promise to pay future income over a designated period that can include — if the contract so designates — the lifetime of the contract holder and a spouse.

The fixed index annuity is a relatively new addition to the annuity family. To understand its development, we need to look at its predecessors, all of which remain intact today and all of which contributed in some fashion to the FIA.

The fixed annuity

Also known as the "fixed-rate annuity," this investment represents one of the earliest types of annuities. Roman soldiers are said to have used a form of fixed annuity to guarantee income after they left Caesar's legions.[23] Fixed annuities offer a guaranteed

---

[23] Fixed annuities became even more popular during the Great Depression when insurance companies provided investment growth and security that many failing banks could not. Part of their legacy is that Babe Ruth used them to successfully protect his baseball income from the ravages of the Depression.

interest rate with all interest in the account growing on a tax-deferred basis. They also offer protection against loss of principal.

A fixed annuity is a contract you purchase from an insurance company that guarantees the interest rate to be generated on the principal you pay. That interest rate typically increases when the insurance company holds your money over a longer period of time during the accumulation period. After that period expires, the contract owner can — among other options — begin receiving regular payments from the insurance company at whatever payout rate the contract guarantees. Those payments can span however long a time period you designate in the contract — a period that can include your lifetime and that of a spouse.

The insurance company invests your premium primarily in U.S. treasuries and highly rated corporate bonds. Its goal is to produce a guaranteed interest rate over the accumulation period set by the contract. The ability to produce a guaranteed rate is a risk taken solely by the insurance company.

Upon the expiration of the accumulation period, the contract owner has several options, depending on how the contract is structured. One might take all principal and accumulated interest in a lump-sum payment. One can roll over the new account value into a new annuity or renew the original annuity at a new interest rate for an additional period of time. Or, one can exercise the above-mentioned option of beginning a payout period in which regular payments are received for however long is designated in the contract.

Note that even a fixed annuity has a surrender period in which you will pay a penalty for early withdrawal of your money. The surrender period is reduced over time, as is the percentage of penalty amount. On a more positive note, many fixed annuities offer a limited opportunity for some withdrawal of principal — sometimes as much as 10 percent a year — without penalty during the surrender period.

Note, too, that fixed annuities once paid a considerably higher interest rate when interest rates were higher. Those rates have fallen considerably in the low-inflation, low-interest climate that followed the Great Recession.

The immediate annuity

Also known as the "single-premium immediate annuity," this financial tool turns a lump-sum premium payment into an immediate stream of annuitized income payments stretching over however long a period the contract determines. That period can cover the life of the annuitant or even that of a surviving spouse if the contract is structured accordingly.

In explaining this annuity, we first need to talk about "annuitization," the process in which income is taken from an immediate annuity.

When annuitizing an annuity contract, control of the contract passes from the contract holder to the insurance company. A contract holder cannot demand the return of his principal once annuitization has occurred. Once you begin receiving annuitized payments, the process cannot be reversed. You will no longer have access to your money in a lump sum.

At the time of annuitization, the insurance company promises to make regular income payments for as long as the contract stipulates.

If you choose in your contract to receive payments for the rest of your life, the insurance company will use actuarial tables to determine how long you might be expected to live. The company then uses that estimate, as well as the value of your contract, to determine what you will receive in each regular payment. If you live longer than the company estimated, the company might eventually pay out more than the contract's actual value. But, should you die sooner than expected, the insurance company retains whatever is left of the contract value.

That last prospect is one reason people sometimes balk at the lifetime payments option of an immediate annuity. Some opt instead for a "period certain" payout. A contract holder might choose, say, a "10-year period certain" payout in which the insurance company is obligated to pay someone — either the annuitant or a beneficiary(s) — payments for 10 years even if the annuitant dies three years into the period. All payments end at the end of the 10-year period.

Also available on some contract is a "life with period certain" option that requires the insurance company to make payments to the annuitant for life but also to a beneficiary(s) should the annuitant die during the specified time. Example: Joe's annuity has a "life with 10 years certain" payout. Joe dies four years after payments begin. His designated beneficiary(s) will continue to receive his payments for the remaining six years of the 10-year period.

The idea of giving up control of your money is part of the reason annuitization is not used as much today as it once was. Modern contracts on other annuity products offer alternative ways to take income that do not involve relinquishing control of the contract. We'll talk about "income riders" and other income-taking alternatives in our upcoming discussion of taking income from annuities.

Still, for a consumer wishing to turn a lump sum amount of money — say, from a 401(k) rollover, a life insurance benefit, an inheritance, the sale of a home or business or (dare we say it?) a winning lottery ticket — into a long-standing stream of contractually guaranteed income, the immediate annuity remains an option.

The variable annuity

The variable annuity (VA) was introduced in the mid-1950s as an alternative to fixed annuities.

It is sold by insurance companies only through persons registered to sell investment products. This is because, in a variable annuity contract, the insurance company is actually investing your money in the stock or bond market where it is subject to gains and losses. Consequently, a variable annuity contract value has an opportunity to grow more than a fixed annuity, but it also could lose value during periods of market declines.

The insurance company's market investments are made through "sub accounts" that resemble mutual funds in the way they reflect different market sectors and different levels of risk tolerance. The VA investor in most contracts can pick from among a multitude of sub-accounts.

As is also the case with mutual funds, the value of these sub-accounts will rise and fall depending on how the securities in each sub-account perform each day on the market. The VA contract holder's account balance will rise and fall accordingly.

When the contract holder decides to begin taking income from the VA contract, the insurance company begins making regular payments that are determined by the contract's value when the payout period begins. The amount of each payment is locked in once income payments begin.

Because variable annuities are sold by insurance companies, VA contracts also offer a death benefit. These death benefits vary from contract to contract. In some contracts, the death benefit might be the contract value at the time of the contract holder's death. Other contracts might return the premium in the form of a death benefit. Later in this chapter, we'll talk about other options that, for an additional fee, will pay a beneficiary(s) a minimum or enhanced death benefit.

Also, any gains in the VA account value are tax deferred until income is taken from the account.

As you can see, the VA has many different moving parts that incur investment and administrative fees. Most variable annuities have sub-account management fees, as well as the mortality charge associated with offering a death benefit. There are also optional rider fees that we will discuss here shortly. Consequently, I often hear clients mention concerns about variable annuity fees when we discuss this financial option.

The VA began to fall out of favor somewhat after the dot-com bubble burst from 1999 through 2001 and an extended market downturn severely impacted the contract value of many variable annuities in effect at the time.

Yet the VA remains an option for some people today, especially after new options have been added that can guarantee income or other benefits even if the variable annuity's fluctuating contract value is greatly reduced by a major market decline. Many VA contracts today offer — for an additional fee — optional riders that require contractual guarantees from the insurance company. One such "lifetime income rider" might contractually require the company to pay a specified level of lifetime income to the annuitant, regardless of what market performance does to the contract value.

Another "return of premium" rider requires the insurance company pay the annuitant or a beneficiary(s) at least as much as the premium value of the annuity. A death benefit rider might require an enhanced payment be paid to surviving beneficiaries, even if a contract has been annuitized. A "long-term care rider" might provide an amount of money — sometimes as much as twice the principal value of the contract — to help pay for the contract holder's long-term care in a nursing home or assisted living situation. Each of these optional riders comes with a separate fee.

(We'll talk about "income riders" in greater detail later in this chapter.)

In summing up the variable annuity, let's note, while it offers the potential for greater contract value growth through investment in the stock market, it also has no protection against loss of principal due to market fluctuations, and can have a high fee structure. Optional riders that provide contractually guaranteed income or other benefits are available in many VA contracts for those willing to pay extra fees.

The fixed index annuity

The fixed index annuity, or "FIA," offers protection against loss of principal due to market fluctuation, just as a fixed annuity does. It also offers the potential for greater growth than does a fixed annuity, though less potential growth than a variable annuity.

The FIA is somewhat like the VA in that it offers the ability to earn interest tied to the performance of a market index. Unlike the VA, however, the FIA is not directly invested in the market. Rather, the FIA *tracks* the performance of a designated market index — such as the S&P 500, the Dow Jones Industrial Average or any other common stock or bond index — and credits interest to the account based on the performance of that index.

What does this mean to the FIA contract holder?

Well, when the tracked index is experiencing gains, the insurance company calculates interest on your annuity's anniversary date, and credits that interest to your account, subject to a cap or participation rate that we will explain shortly. But, because the contract holder is not directly invested in the securities on the tracked index, his or her account value does not experience a loss if the tracked index undergoes a decline.

To better illustrate the workings of the FIA, let's plug in some hypothetical numbers.

Let's say you use the S&P 500 as the tracking index of your FIA. Now let's say this index increases 7.9 percent during the tracking period designated by the contract. How much of that increase you will receive in interest credited to your account depends on the cap or participation rate included in your contract. If your cap is 5 percent and the S&P 500 gains 7.9 percent, you will receive a 5 percent increase in account value. If the index gain is 3 percent and your cap is 5, you get the full 3 percent in interest.

(We'll explain caps, spreads and participation rates later in this chapter.)

Now, let's say the S&P 500 falls 23 percent (as it did in 2002) or 38.5 percent as happened in 2008 during the middle of the Great Recession. Because your principal is not directly invested in the stock market, you experience no losses when the market does. The insurance company assumes all the risk against loss of principal due to market volatility.

The FIA, in short, has both a ceiling and a floor during the contract's accumulation phase — again, defined as the period of contract growth until you begin taking income from the account.

The "ceiling" is the limit on the amount of tracked index gains for which you will receive index credited interest during each tracking period. Your initial "floor" is the premium you paid for the FIA; your contract value will not fall below that point until you begin receiving payments. Moreover, FIA contracts with annual resets "lock in" interest credits realized from previous years, thus establishing a new floor level whenever interest is credited.

Note, however, that things change once you begin taking income from an FIA.

Your account value will now be reduced by any amount you take in payments. My goal for clients taking income from an FIA is to attempt to balance, as closely as one can, the amount of annual interest credited to the account against the amount taken out for payments. If you can have as much (or almost as much) credited interest coming into the account as you have in payments flowing out, your chance of keeping the FIA alive for an extended period is increased.

Another option when taking income is to consider purchasing an income rider that contractually guarantees income payment even if an FIA's account value reaches $0. (We'll detail this option, as well as other ways of taking income, later in this chapter.)

Caps, participation rates, spreads

Your FIA growth rate is limited by caps, participation rates or spreads — three different concepts that perform the same function. Let's briefly look at each.

A *cap* is what it suggests: a lid on the amount you can realize from an index gain.

Let's say the index crediting method in your FIA is the S&P 500, and it grows 7.5 percent in a year that begins with the anniversary date of your contract. If your contract caps your participation in that growth at 5 percent, a 5 percent interest rate will be credited to your account. A 3.5 percent growth in the index earns you the full 3.5 percent. Conversely, a 5 percent loss in the index will result in no loss to your accumulation value.

A *participation rate* allows you the opportunity to participate in more of the index growth during an especially bullish year.

Let's say your FIA contract allows a 70 percent participation rate and your strategy index, the NASDAQ, rises 10 percent in a good year for tech stocks. The interest generated for your account would be 7 percent. If the NASDAQ index rises only 3.5 percent in your accounting period, you would be credited with only 2.45 percent. Conversely, a 7 percent loss in the index will result in no loss to your accumulation value.

In a *spread* system, the insurance company keeps all gains to the point of the designated spread point, and the contract holder gets anything above it. Again, this approach works best for the owner in times of strong market performance.

Let's say you have a 3.5 percent spread number in your FIA contract that has the Dow Jones Industrial Average as its index strategy. If the Dow rises 10 percent in your accounting period, your gain is 6.5 percent (10 minus 3.5). If, however, the Dow rises only 4 percent, your gain is only 0.5 percent. If the strategy index falls below the spread, the result is the same as if there was a negative return — that is, no gain and no loss for that accounting period.

Insurance companies use caps, participation rates and spreads in FIAs to support the expense they take in guarding against loss of principal during down market times. The use of these limits makes the FIA different from the variable annuity in which a contract holder has full participation — minus fees — in the rise of sub-accounts values. It goes without saying, however, that the VA contract holder also has full participation in all losses in sub-account values.

Note here that insurance companies have the right to adjust, usually annually, their caps, participation rates and spreads. This is because the cost of operating the annuity can change from year-to-year, thus affecting how much of an index change the company needs to keep in order to assume the risk when guaranteeing no loss of principal in a fixed annuity.

Point-to-point accounting periods can affect your gain

I occasionally have a client bring an annual FIA account statement to my office and wonder why the growth in their index strategy didn't match the actual growth in the index itself.

"Bruce," they might say, "I see all these year-end news stories about how the S&P 500 had a 6 percent gain for the year. Now, I know I'm capped at 5 percent, but my statement shows my gain for the year at only 3.5 percent. What gives?"

Well, I might say after a closer look, it seems like one bad month last year was especially awful for you.

This happens occasionally when a client's interest for a year is calculated using an annual point-to-point method, a very common practice in many FIAs.

The year-long accounting period using this method is a 365-day stretch that usually coincides with the anniversary date of the contract. If the anniversary day is Nov. 1, the insurance company will read the S&P 500 index on that day and compare to the index on Oct. 31 of the following year. If there was a significant market blip in, say, October, it could turn an otherwise productive year into only a 3.5 percent gain, down from the 6 percent hike the index realized from Jan. 1 through Dec. 31 — the media counting period — after it rebounded from its October swoon.

Annual point-to-point accounting is only one of several methods used to determine the yearly interest to be credited to your FIA account.

A monthly point-to-point system can, in very bullish years, produce some significant returns.

In this method, interest is calculated each month on a capped basis. A typical cap rate is 1.5 percent growth each month, meaning if you're fortunate enough to have 12 winning months, you could see an 18 percent gain in a year (12 months x 1.5 percent per month).

Such a year is rare, however. It's not unusual to see one or two bad months knock the legs out from under 10 good ones. Example: The S&P 500 is on a roll from January through the end of April. You've posted a 1.5 percent gain in each of the year's first four months and are sitting on a 6 percent cumulative increase at the start of May. But May is an awful month, and the S&P 500 is down 4 percent. Your gain for the year to date is reset at only 2 percent.

Other accounting periods include monthly and even daily averaging of your strategy index. The insurance company will take the average of 12 months of index performance, or 365 days if that's your choice, and determine the index growth for the year. It then applies your cap/spread/participation rate to the formula and computes your total rate of interest growth for the year. It's important to note that no one crediting method will perform best in every market scenario.

The benefits of the FIA with annual reset

OK, enough of the somewhat technical explanation of the inner workings of annuities. Let's look at how an FIA can work in various market conditions.

For the purpose of this exercise, let's say we have a hypothetical FIA, with interest crediting tied to the performance of the S&P 500 index. We start with a $200,000 base value. The historical rise and fall of the S&P 500 in each of the years shown here is used to demonstrate how the FIA's annual reset feature works.

For the purpose of this example, let's further assume the FIA contract caps the participation in index-credited interest to 5 percent each year. In 1998, the S&P 500 rose by roughly 26 percent (from 1/1/1998-12/31/1998).

In this case, the FIA would have potentially earned interest of 5 percent, with its accumulation/cash account value rising to $210,000. A year later the index rose another 19.5 percent — glory days, indeed — and the contract's value could have increased another 5 percent to $220,500.

At this point, you might think, "Well, that FIA isn't doing as well as the index. The S&P 500 is soared to new heights, but the FIA only received a small portion of that."

Well, you're not wrong, but look one year later, when the dot-com bubble burst. The index plummeted in 2000 by 10 percent, then dropped again in 2001 and '02 by another 13 and 23 percent respectively.

How would the look at this point?

Actually, pretty good. Its contract value would have remained steady after taking no losses in previously locked-in interest during three years of market turmoil. The index, meanwhile, took the big downward ride.

In 2008, in one of the greatest market downturns since the Great Depression, the S&P 500 index dropped 38.5 percent. However, due to the FIA's guaranteed floor and annual reset feature, its value wouldn't drop, despite the economic turmoil.

Bottom line, the FIA doesn't have to make up for any losses due to market declines along the way, all because of the power of annual reset. Of course, this example doesn't include fees and expenses, and also assumes that the cap is a steady 5 percent throughout, which is not likely. An FIA's limitations, such as caps, spreads and participation rates, are subject to change throughout the life of the annuity, making it difficult to look back and see exactly how an FIA could have performed. However, this does give you an idea as to how the FIA can react to shifts in the market, both positive and negative.

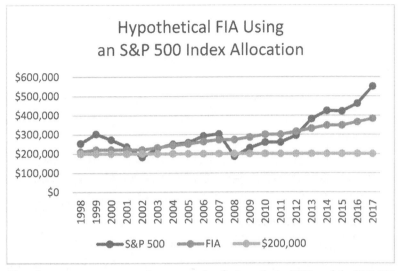

This chart represents past performance only of a hypothetical FIA and the S&P 500 index and may not be used to predict future results. The $200,000 line assumes no interest credited in all years. Your actual results will vary

Keep in mind that it may be possible to reallocate your FIA index strategies at various times throughout the life of the annuity to anticipate different market conditions. Because no one crediting method will perform best in every market, you have the ability to change your crediting method (as permitted by your contract) if you choose to potentially take advantage of future market conditions.

For example: You might leave 20 percent of the FIA value in an index strategy with a cap while putting 80 percent in another un-capped index strategy with a spread or participation rate, which have the potential to produce a more aggressive interest rate. Obviously, there is no guarantee of this, and again, no one index strategy will perform best in every market scenario. However, it gives you a better idea of how the FIA with annual reset could work in a volatile and unpredictable market.

The choice of which route you choose to take in retirement is entirely up to you, of course. An account of purely market-based investments has the potential to outperform an annuity over a long period of time but comes with the potential for loss as well. It's an approach many investors can afford to pursue at younger times of their lives.

The concern for people in retirement, however, is that you don't know if you've got 20 years to see if a market-based investment portfolio might perform like the one earlier.

This can be especially problematic when you begin taking income from such a portfolio, something you will begin to do in retirement when you become voluntarily unemployed. If you are dependent on income from investments tied strictly to the shifting winds of the stock market, bear markets such as 2008, or 2000-02, or 1973-74, among others, can cause great distress.

Can you live with this kind of uncertainty in retirement? Some people can, and more power to them. But as a personal observation based on years of dealing with retirement-age clients, I find many people at this stage of life have less of an appetite for the wild ups and downs that can come with a purely market-based portfolio.

What I hear often from retirement-age clients is that conservative, steady growth with a guarantee of no loss of principal or previously locked-in interest credits is a preferred way of preserving at least a portion of their retirement assets.

This is why I'm such a big believer in the potential benefits of the fixed index annuity and its place in at least part of a well-balanced retirement nest egg for many retirees and pre-retirees.

Taking income from annuities

Growing your account value over a period of several years in the accumulation phase of an annuity is only half the story. Your reward for doing so comes when you decide to begin the distribution or "payout" phase, the point where you begin taking income from the contract.

I'm talking here about taking regular income payments from an annuity, something considerably different than the option in some contracts that allows you to withdraw as much as 10 percent of your invested principal even during the surrender period.

There are three basics methods for taking income from an annuity.

Annuitization

I described the annuitization process earlier in our discussion on immediate annuities, so I won't repeat too much of it here. But let's briefly recap some main points.

Annuitization turns control of the annuity contract over to the insurance company, which promises, in turn, to make regular income payments over a period designated by the contract holder. This period can be for the lifetime of the annuitant and often a surviving spouse, the "life with survivor" option. It also can be for "life with period certain," meaning that, should the annuitant die shortly after first receiving payments, a beneficiary(s) will continue to receive those payments for the remainder of the designated period. Payments also can be made over a defined "period certain" number of years. Again, all these payout options are described in the immediate annuity section above.

Keep in mind, too, that in the case of a "life only" or "life with survivor" payout schedule, any money remaining in the annuitized contract after the death of the annuitant and surviving spouse belongs to the insurance company. Heirs can benefit only when "period certain" is a part of the payout option.

The annuitization of contracts is not used nearly as much today — indeed, I would say "rarely used" — largely because of other income-taking options that do not involve turning over control of the contract to the insurance company. Let's spend our time looking at these options.

Systematic withdrawals

You need to know a contract holder can take some penalty-free withdrawals from an FIA at any time after the first year, and those withdrawals can usually be up to 10 percent of the current contract value. Such systematic withdrawals can be made on a monthly, quarterly or annual basis.

Once the surrender period of an annuity contract is over, the contract holder has full control of withdrawals on a penalty-free basis. The contract holder can even withdraw the entire accumulated amount — premiums and interest — in a lump sum payout, though this defeats our intended purpose of using an annuity to provide a long-time stream of income.

Note that the accumulation/cash value of the annuity will decline with each withdrawal, and the account value could drop to $0 over time. But, because the accumulation pool in an FIA can continue to experience index growth even after payouts begin, a contract holder whose systematic withdrawals stay close to, or only slightly above, the growth level of the contract can reasonably expect to keep the contract intact for an extended period. By doing this, you are creating a controlled level of reduction with no exposure to market risk.

Hypothetical example: Many financial advisors base retirement income planning on the "4 percent rule," which has historically been something of an industry standard for the amount of money one can reasonably expect to take in annual income from retirement accounts. But what if you need more than 4 percent to live on? Withdrawing 4 percent each year from a $100,000 portfolio produces around $4,000 a year. What if you need $5,000?

The index growth of an FIA can give you the potential and opportunity to take more than the conventional 4 percent without fear of running out of money.

Using a typical FIA contract with a contract value of $100,000, let's say we want to take $5,000 annually as income. If the index strategy of the contract averages a 5 percent return a year, our example accumulation value would be $112,634 after 20 years.

Let's examine how we arrived at those figures.

Since we have to defer most contracts for the first year — meaning we can't take any withdrawals in Year One — the accumulated value after Year One is $105,000 after an average 5 percent return on $100,000. In Year Two you start taking $5,000 from the contract at the same time the index strategy is growing the contract by about that same amount. Compounding the interest annually will accumulate additional value over our example 20-year period.

End result: Because your contract is growing faster than you're draining it, you are creating the opportunity to either leave money for your family or increase your income later in life as your needs change, such as if you require long-term nursing care. Keep in mind, this example is hypothetical only. It is highly unlikely, if not impossible, for a product to average a 5 percent interest credit every year. There will be years with 0 percent interest, just as well as some years that could provide more than 5 percent in interest.

But what you are attempting to do, in effect, is create a sustainable income. Rather than living on the 4 percent rule, you can have the opportunity to adjust your income as your needs change. This is a privilege few people have.

Because this method of taking income payments does not involve annuitization, any money remaining in the contract can be passed on to heirs following the death of the annuitant and a surviving spouse.

This method of taking income is typically used by people who do not want to annuitize a contract or elect not to pay the added expense of the optional "income rider" that assures the continuance of income payments even if the accumulation value of a contract reaches $0.

The coming of the "income rider"

An income rider is an option — added onto a contract for an annual fee — that requires the insurance company to pay you and/or a spouse income for life.

To better understand how this optional income rider provides the opportunity for lifetime income, picture an FIA with separate values.

One is the accumulation/cash value figure common to all FIAs. This value has the potential to grow as it does in all FIAs, through either fixed interest, index-credited interest or a combination of the two. This value begins to decrease when income payments begin, and fees for optional riders also are deducted here. The cash value in this situation is money that can be withdrawn in a lump sum if desired — presumably after the surrender period has passed — or passed on to heirs if any cash remains after payouts begin.

The other value is commonly known as the "income account value."

This figure is not cash; you can't withdraw money from it when you suddenly need to finance a home repair or pay a hospital bill. Think of the numbers here as credits that will be used to determine how much the insurance company will pay out in regular installments for the remainder of your life once you elect to begin receiving income. The insurance company is obligated to make lifetime payments based on this "income account value" even if the accumulation/cash value runs out of money after you begin receiving payments.

This income value side often grows annually at a fixed rate based on the premium paid. The income rider fee on many contracts as of this writing is usually around 1–1.5 percent or more of the premium paid. It's not a cheap option. Moreover, different insurance companies vary in the way they assess the income rider fee. Some compute it as a percentage of the accumulation account, others on the income account value side. These calculations can make a significant difference in the accumulated value of the annuity.

Still, the guaranteed growth of the income value has the potential to exceed that of the accumulation side, which consequently could produce a larger pool of interest credits than is generated in cash on the accumulation side. This is not always the case, and there can be instances after an extended bull market where the accumulation/cash value side might be greater than the income value side.

The insurance company uses this income figure — as opposed to the accumulation/cash value — to determine the dollar amount of each regular payout.[24] Actuarial tables are used to calculate the size of the monthly, quarterly or annual payouts you will receive. The main factors in that calculation are the age of the annuitants and the size of the income value.

Another optional rider in many annuities — again, available for an added charge — provides a minimum guaranteed death benefit. This death benefit is usually equal to or slightly more than the premium paid to purchase the annuity. The death benefit gives a beneficiary a chance to immediately receive a larger payout than the accumulation/cash side might provide. If a death benefit is taken,

---

[24] At the point in life when you elect to take guaranteed income payments without annuitization, doing so from the income rider, if the accumulation value is higher than the income account value, your guaranteed income payment will be based on the higher of the two values.

however, the insurance company no longer is obligated to make regular guaranteed income payments.

One final note: Many income account riders offer additional liquidity in the event of long-term care confinement or diagnosis of a terminal illness.

Slow and steady can win the race

The conservative, steady growth potential of the FIA suggests accurately that this isn't a high growth product. Though it does offer the potential for index-credited interest, it is designed instead to produce steady income.

As we briefly mentioned earlier, some people will seek more interest than the FIA provides. That's fine for those comfortable with taking a risk, and there is always a place for some element of risk even in the most conservative of retirement portfolios. We'll talk more in a later chapter about choosing to play on Wall Street.

But for those seeking principal protection and competitive interest credit opportunity in their retirement savings, the FIA can offer both.

I understand annuities may not be for everyone, and I would not suggest that you want your entire retirement savings allocated there. You will, for instance, need a source of cash or other invested capital that you can access quickly for emergency situations or even retirement dreams. An annuity is not intended to serve that "quick cash" purpose. Additionally, few assets can help address inflation better than those tied to the market.

At the same time, however, you also must realize your financial priorities change as you approach or enter retirement. Your objectives are different as you transition from the growth/accumulation phase of life (referred to as "investment planning") to the distribution/income phase, also known as "retirement planning." Your objectives now become primarily principal protection, sustainable income, the flexibility of choices and, yes, growth. Your investment plan must now transition into a retirement plan, which means you also need to change your tools. The annuity is one such tool to help you get that job done.

With the decline in company-sponsored defined benefit pension plans, developing an income plan that produces the income you know you can count on — income to supplement that of Social Security and any other monthly income you might receive — is essential. As I mentioned earlier, no other financial product can promise a consistent flow of regular income like an annuity can.

The rules governing annuities can sometimes be complicated, and an insurance professional you trust should take whatever time is necessary to explain your options. But don't let the complexities scare you off.

Instead, ask yourself this: How scary was it to live through the volatility and anxiety and uncertainty of the Great Recession from late 2007 through the spring of 2009? How would you handle a similar market downturn now that you are retired? How prepared are you to deal with such a possibility when you're in a fixed income situation?

One final question: Why even consider the possibility of fluctuations in value for your basic income expenses when you don't have to? Why do that when you have an available option that can protect large parts of your retirement savings from loss, and thus offering you the courage to retire?

CHAPTER 8

Living with Mistakes in Retirement

We've all made our share of mistakes in life. We'll likely make even more before the inevitable day comes when we can no longer make them.

Having made my share of miscues, I've come to believe that the key to dealing with them is to pick ourselves up after making one, then learning something from what we did wrong — or what someone else did wrong — that keeps us from doing the same dumb thing twice.

Let's try to learn something, for example, from the story of a friend of mine whom I will call Dan, a made-up name for a real person.

Upon entering early retirement at age 55, Dan rolled most of his 401(k) money, about $896,000, into a personal IRA with significant exposure to the stock market. He did this in early 2007. I don't think I have to remind you what happened to the market starting later that year and into the spring of 2009.

Did Dan make a mistake in doing this? I believe he did, though not necessarily for the reason you might imagine.

Yes, Dan's IRA took a major thrashing during the Great Recession when it lost more than half its value. Even so, I don't see Dan's mistake as being *when* he invested. He was a victim of bad luck in his timing, to be sure, but the overall market trend had been positive when he opened his moderately aggressive brokerage account in early 2007.

Rather, I see Dan's mistake in being *how* he invested in early 2007.

Had he invested at least a portion of his IRA funds into a fixed index annuity or other principal protected financial vehicle, Dan would have had that portion of his IRA in a financial product that offered protection against loss of principal during times of market volatility, which the Great Recession certainly was. When the stock market recovery began in 2009, he could have experienced conservative growth.

OK, I can imagine what you're saying. Looking at what should have been done is easy today with the benefit of 20-20 hindsight. And it's true that only a few insiders had the vision back then to foresee the bursting of the mortgage-backed securities bubble that precipitated the start of the Great Recession. Again, that's why I can't be too critical of Dan for *when* he made his big move.

But it's equally true that he might have helped himself in *how* he made his big investment, especially at an all-important time in his life when he was entering semi-retirement.

I wish I'd been his financial advisor in 2007, when we would have talked about the dangers of putting too much retirement money — money you simply can't afford to lose at this stage of your life — into Wall Street. I wish we could have talked then about how protection of at least a portion of one's retirement money should be a primary focus for financial decisions made in the years just before retirement.

Fortunately for Dan, his was not a fatal mistake. He still had some time at age 55 to recover before he planned to begin taking income from his IRA account somewhere around age 70.

This is what I mean by living with mistakes in retirement. To be sure, there will be dips in the road leading into and through retirement. But with proper planning, these potholes need not leave you broken down by the side of the road. Learning from our mistakes, as well as the common mistakes of others, can help provide a clearer view of the road ahead and possibly keep you from steering directly into trouble that might otherwise be avoided.

I see a lot of avoidable mistakes made by people approaching or in retirement. Let's talk about some of the more common ones.

Mistake 1: Too much retirement money in one place

I see this happen most commonly in a company-sponsored 401(k) where the company's stock is a primary investment option or the other investment options are limited.

When you have too much of your retirement portfolio in any one or two securities — or even in a small handful of securities — it can cause your anxiety meter to rise to red-line levels if your primary holdings experience a major market-related downturn. This is especially true when you are approaching or are in retirement, and you are preparing to take (or are actively taking) income from those stocks or mutual funds. Keep in mind that unless you can live off just the dividends produced by these holdings, you will have to sell shares of your stocks or funds to produce the income you desire. And selling shares of stock at a reduced price is hardly an effective way to produce income.

Here in my home area of southwest Missouri we recently saw that kind of anxiety turn into something close to panic selling when the stock price of a well-regarded local company experienced a significant decline.

The XYZ Company — a fictional name for a real company — is a major employer in the region. Its stock is a major component of the company's 401(k) plan. Many of its employees are happy to have this option, as they believe in the company and its long-term future. But even this rock-solid faith began to crack when the company's stock price took a major hit, the result of a nationally prominent investor's comments on the sector in which XYZ operates.

XYZ was motoring along nicely at or near a 52-week high of around $285 a share before this analyst predicted an industry-wide downturn in future sales and growth. In a short period of time, XYZ lost some 44 percent of its market value, its price plummeting to a 52-week low in the $155 range.

XYZ employees with large holdings of the company stock in their 401(k) plans and years to go until retirement typically held tight during the downturn. They believed in the company they worked for, saw its overall future as bright and held onto their XYZ stock in the belief that it would rebound. Good for them, as the stock eventually did exactly that.

"Holding the line" wasn't so easy, however, for employees nearing retirement. It was even harder for retired employees who retained their XYZ holdings either in their 401(k)s or in personal IRAs created by a 401(k) rollover.

These folks also liked and believed in the company, but they also were either about to be, or were dependent on, XYZ stock for income. Actively taking income from a stock experiencing a price plunge typically results in slowing the flow of that income. (Either that or you must sell more shares to produce the same level of income.) Not knowing how far the stock price might plummet prompted some to sell most or even all XYZ shares in an attempt to stop the bleeding and preserve whatever market value they had remaining.

When the stock price started a slow recovery, many of the people who sold large portions of their holdings began to suspect they had made a big mistake in panic-selling at the bottom range of the XYZ price plunge. Some tried to recover by buying back shares at a higher price. They lost money in the short term but hoped to make it back over the long run.

Did these good folks make a mistake in selling at or near the stock's low point? In hindsight we have to say "yes," especially when considering the stock price rebound that followed over the ensuing weeks and months.

Yet, we have to add a qualifier here.

I understand why these folks did what they did. I really do. The anxiety is intense when any one security upon which you are dependent for retirement income experiences a dramatic loss in value. You turn the tourniquet even tighter to stop the bleeding.

I also understand their initial mistake need not be devastating. This is especially true for those who bought back shares during the price rebound and slowly began to reclaim some of what they lost.

There is a lesson to be learned here, albeit at the expense of others.

"Panic selling" is never good, especially in retirement. You lose too much of your investment, and your time frame to recover from that loss is now limited.

The key here is to offset some of the circumstances that can induce panic selling. Maintaining a diversified portfolio of investments — nothing too heavy in any one or two positions — is one essential step.

A more important one, I would argue, is something I've been emphasizing throughout this book.

I've said this before, but it bears repeating. There is room in a retirement portfolio for some degree of risk as a means of realizing a greater return. That risk can be better handled emotionally, however, when one knows his or her retirement income isn't based solely on market-exposed investments.

Here is where a flow of contractually guaranteed income — Social Security, pension payments, regular income payments from annuities — is so valuable. This "mailbox income" gives you the courage to know you will have a stream of income that is steady and reliable, even if Wall Street tanks like it did during the Great Recession, or as XYZ's stock did briefly after an analyst's comment.

Mistake 2: Spending too much too soon

I've seen it happen far too often.

People retire and immediately set out to live the retirement lifestyle they've heard about and envisioned for themselves. They buy a boat, they buy a vacation condo, they travel to exotic places. They spend a lot of money, then five years later they grow tired of the travel and start thinking about other things they'd like to do.

The trouble is, they now have a lot less money to do those other things than they had when they retired.

Did they make a mistake? Maybe, maybe not.

Again, how you spend your retirement savings is entirely up to you. Only you know your retirement priorities, and if travel and recreation are high atop that list, who's to say you're wrong in going for it?

Unless, that is, you begin to worry years later that you are now in danger of outliving the pool of money you once thought would last for the rest of your life. When you find yourself wondering if you can afford to attend a grandson's college graduation or a granddaughter's wedding in some distant state, the good life you thought you were living suddenly doesn't seem so grand anymore. It all comes down to budgeting, which in retirement means doing many of the same things you did in your working years. The major difference, of course, is that you are now on a fixed income.

Still, you budget for your regular monthly household expenses. You make an allowance for dining out and entertainment. You set resources aside for emergency needs and health care. You then balance these known expenses against your known monthly income, making adjustments where necessary on either side of the expense/income equation.

Only when this basic budgeting is done will you know what you can afford for nonessential expenses that are nonetheless important to you. Only then will you know if you can buy a bass boat, take that dream vacation to the south of France or own a winter condo in Arizona. Or, if the budget numbers aren't what you had hoped, perhaps you consider alternatives — a trip instead to south Florida, or a two-week winter rental in Scottsdale.

Budgeting for retirement dreams becomes easier when you grow a pool of guaranteed monthly income from Social Security and pension payments, including the income stream you can establish for yourself through annuities. Knowing you have enough "mailbox income" to meet fixed monthly expenses allows you to consider the option of taking income from other retirement investments to spend on retirement dreams.

Mistake 3: Not fully understanding your retirement savings tools

You've been saving all your life for retirement. You get quarterly statements from different firms showing account values that verify you have assets. Congratulations on your good work to this point.

Now, do you fully understand how to turn these investment assets into income?

Sadly, many people don't. Equally sad is how some advisors who were very helpful in selling investment products aren't nearly as helpful when it comes time to take income from those products. This is very unfortunate, as taking income in a strategic manner is one of the most important things you will do in retirement.

Look, if you're going to put part of your life savings in any investment tool, you darn sure need to know exactly how that tool works. And yet, too many people don't fully understand how much annual income they can take from, say, an annuity they've been growing for years, or how much they should expect to take from a market-based investment without completely depleting the asset.

During the investment stage of life, these issues probably aren't especially important to you. Your priority then is growth, growth, growth. Your financial advisor, whose compensation is sometimes based on the growth in your accounts, has a vested interest in seeing you achieve that growth.

But your objectives change in retirement. Your investment plan must now become a retirement income plan from which you will draw the money you need to live on for the rest of your life. As these objectives change, so too does the financial tools you will use — specifically, those that turn your assets into lifelong income while still providing some potential for further growth.

You guessed it, I'm advocating again for the fixed index annuity that provides guarantees against the loss of principal while offering the potential for interest credits based in part on the performance of a market index. When an optional income rider is added to such an annuity, the insurance company is contractually obligated to make income payments to the annuitant for life. Even without this income rider option, the index-based interest growth potential in the FIA's cash value could allow an annuitant to take income from the account for many years, often a period covering the rest of that person's life.

But just buying an annuity isn't enough.

You also need to know exactly how and when this annuity will pay you income. How long must you own the annuity contract before you can begin taking income? How long is the contract's surrender period, and what are the penalties for withdrawals taken during this period? What do income withdrawals do to account value, and what are the chances of this account value falling to $0? What is the difference between the "income/benefit" side and the "account value" side of an annuity with an income rider? Can any unused part of an annuity be passed on to heirs?

I addressed some of these questions in the preceding chapter, but the important thing to note here is that you simply have to discuss these questions with your financial advisor.

Have him or her produce a written plan that projects how much annual income each asset in your portfolio will produce. In dealing with your market-based brokerage investments, discuss the percentage you can reasonably take as annual income without completely depleting the asset. Again, your goal is to withdraw for income only as much (or just slightly more, if necessary) than the asset is growing, and that value might occasionally change as market conditions do.

Also important: Understand which of your investments are tied directly to market performance, as well as which are protected from market declines. Remember the sub-accounts in variable annuities reflect daily market fluctuations that can create solid gains as well as substantial losses. Ask whether adding an income rider — which guarantees a lifelong payment of income even if the account value of the variable annuity falls to $0 — is a viable option for such an annuity.

Having a full understanding of how each financial tool in your retirement portfolio works — the risk level involved, and how each will produce income — is a key to avoiding mistakes during this new period of life.

Mistake 4: Gambling on Medicare alone to cover your health expenses

Just as Social Security was never intended to provide all income in retirement, neither was Medicare intended to cover all medical expenses in retirement.

I believe the vast majority of people either about to take Medicare or who are actively within the program understand basic Medicare at best will pay only 80 percent of health care expenses. I also believe many of these people also understand the purpose of optional Medicare supplement plans that pay some or even all of what Medicare does not cover.

Even so, I still come across people who think they can get through retirement on Medicare alone. They believe they have the resources to pay the bills that Medicare does not and thus can avoid the additional cost of supplemental insurance coverage.

Is this a mistake? Well, even if you don't want to call it that, it is a pretty big gamble. While no one is required to buy a Medicare supplement plan — or Medicare Advantage as a cost-control alternative to traditional Medicare — there are risks taken in not doing so.

The risk is not so much to one's health as it is to one's personal wealth — that is, the retirement savings you expect to live on for the rest of your life. Let's look at that a little more closely.

Let's say you've got a $200,000 pool of retirement money from which you plan to supplement monthly income received from Social Security and any other source. Now, let's say you need an emergency heart surgery. You learn afterward that you have $40,000 to $50,000 in unpaid bills, your 20 percent of the costs that Medicare did not cover. This one major surgery or catastrophic illness has quickly taken 25 percent or more from your life savings. It's easy to see why health care expenses are a major factor in bankruptcies involving seniors. Keep in mind that, even with Medicare, after the deductibles and copays, there is no ceiling on one's out-of-pocket medical expenses.

Among the things we know with something close to absolute certainty — just behind death and taxes — is that our health will deteriorate as we get older. Because we don't live a Benjamin Button existence — the mythical character who was born elderly and grew younger as he aged — we know our health care costs are only going to rise as we go deeper into retirement. And while I fervently hope all readers of this book are fortunate enough to go through life without a major illness or need for expensive surgery, we know that's not realistic.

That's why it becomes essential for people approaching age 65 — the time at which we are automatically enrolled in Medicare — to study and understand their options in order to make an educated decision about the kind of health care coverage they will take into retirement. I looked at many of these options in my Chapter 5 discussion on health care in retirement, but I want to revisit a few of the most important options here again.

Medicare supplemental insurance plans — as well as Medicare Advantage plans — are among these options. These plans can get somewhat complicated with different levels of deductibles and coverage, but the bottom line is you will pay a higher premium for supplement plans that provide the most coverage and limit your out-of-pocket expenses. The decision on which option might be best for you and your family will be based on what you think you might need and what you can afford.

Note these plans are offered by a multitude of different insurance companies, many of which will flood your mailbox with introductory pamphlets around the time of open enrollment each fall. I find the easiest way to navigate through the torrent of offers is to consult with a professional who will help you find a plan that best fits your specific needs and budget. I'm proud to say I have my own such person here at The Resource Center in Skip Wilson, our senior services manager. While Skip isn't affiliated with the U.S. government or any government agency, he does have years of dealing with Medicare and Medigap issues both as a consumer and an advisor.

A cautionary note to be made here, one many people may not realize.

People choosing the Medicare Advantage option — a no- or low-premium plan in which participating insurance companies are appointed to administer Medicare by providing Medicare-approved coverage through a cost-controlling network of physicians and medical facilities — might experience difficulty should they elect to switch from an Advantage plan to a supplement plan. Such a person will likely have to qualify medically before being deemed eligible for the change. This is a potential drawback to be discussed with a knowledgeable Medicare counselor such as Skip in advance of making your decision.

Let's also note that people choosing Medicare Advantage must continue to pay Part B premiums, just as do people buying Medicare supplemental plans. These Advantage plans pay the provider directly instead of paying Medicare, and most Advantage Plans also include Part D coverage.[25]

Again, a major part of finding the courage to retire is understanding how to deal with the roadblocks to retirement. Health care costs are a huge, huge roadblock. Part of the path around that obstacle involves deferring the high cost of a catastrophic illness onto an insurance carrier rather than paying for what Medicare doesn't out of your own pocket. The challenge here is to protect your retirement savings, and one way to do that is with a Medicare supplement plan.

But I've also known people who've gotten by in retirement without using supplemental coverage. They set aside a portion — sometimes a rather large portion — of their retirement accounts specifically for health care. Funding health care in retirement can be done that way, but it can be a tough way to do it.

---

[25] Part D prescription drug coverage is not included in basic Medicare or is a component of Medicare supplement plans. It is an optional add-on plan offered by any number of insurance companies. Part D coverage is, however, included in most Medicare Advantage plans.

Opting out of Part B coverage

I've also known people who go even further and exercise their option to opt out of Medicare Part B coverage, either on a temporary or permanent basis. This, I believe, is a mistake and a potential disaster for your future financial security, especially for people who believe they have Medicare coverage they may not actually have.

Let's examine that in more detail. Medicare has two main components, Part A and Part B.

Part A, which covers hospital costs when you are an "admitted" patient, is provided at no additional premium. You paid for this coverage through the Medicare taxes deducted from your payroll checks throughout your working years.

People often fail to understand the significance of being "admitted" to a hospital as opposed to being held for "observation." "Admitted" means you are being hospitalized when determined "medically necessary" by your primary care physician. Medicare Part A coverage applies only to "admitted" patients regardless of the length of their stay.

This distinction becomes significant again should you need rehabilitation in a skilled nursing facility. In this case, to qualify for Part A coverage, you must have been an "admitted" hospital patient for a period of three days deemed "medically necessary" by your primary care physician. Medicare defines a "three-day period" as one that includes overnight stays of at least three midnights.

Medicare Part A *does not* cover hospital expenses when you are held for observation; you must be an "admitted" patient to receive Part A coverage. However, hospital charges when you are held for "observation" are covered by Medicare Part B. These charges can be significant, which is part of why I believe opting out of Part B coverage — as well as not maintaining a supplemental policy to cover some or all of the 20 percent of costs not covered by Part B — is a mistake.

Part B covers — after annual deductibles are met — 80 percent of everything classified as "outpatient" expenses. This coverage for physicians and other health care providers comes with a monthly premium, the full amount of which was $134 in 2018. This amount is typically deducted from one's monthly Social Security benefit. People not yet taking Social Security but who want Part B coverage pay that premium out-of-pocket directly to Medicare, which bills quarterly in typical situations.

Part B coverage has some options with which not everyone is familiar.

A person can opt out of Part B coverage as long as they have what Medicare calls "credible coverage" from some other source. "Credible coverage" is defined as health care coverage that includes at least as much as that provided by Medicare Part B. This often is coverage provided by an employer's group health insurance plan. A person who continues to work beyond the time they become eligible for Medicare can use this coverage as an alternative to Part B and thus avoid paying the Part B premium.

The mistake comes when people opt out of Part B without having this alternative "credible coverage." They do this for various reasons. Maybe they think they don't yet need the coverage. Maybe they just balk at paying the additional premium.

What many of these people don't understand, however, is that they may ultimately pay a penalty for this decision. For, should they someday decide they want to enroll in Part B — and many eventually come to that point as their health deteriorates over time — they will pay the penalty not just for the years they opted out of Part B coverage, but also for all future years they will receive it.

People who opt out of Part B while having "credible coverage" elsewhere do not pay this penalty should they decide to enroll in Part B, which often happens when they leave a job and lose their alternative health care coverage. These people should remember, however, that Part B enrollment is only available at certain times of the year and becomes effective only after a waiting period. An exception is made for people who are losing their "credible coverage." If that is the case, enrollment in Part B becomes effective immediately with no waiting period.

I don't see this often, but I have known people who thought they could avoid Part B premiums until they absolutely needed the coverage. Only then were they surprised to learn of the penalty added on to the normal premium, an extra $50 or $60 a month that they will pay for the rest of their lives.

Mistake 5: Do-it-yourself Medicaid qualification

I understand why people often feel the need to qualify for Medicaid assistance to help pay for long-term care or nursing home confinement.

What I don't understand is why they attempt such a complicated process without expert assistance.

I discussed the Medicaid qualification process in an earlier chapter, so I won't spend a lot of space repeating it here. Let's just note for the record that it can be a very involved process that requires qualified legal assistance, and I'm not a lawyer.

Even so, I'm not rendering a legal opinion when I say it makes me sad to see the mistakes many people make in seeking Medicaid qualification. Especially when these are mistakes that might have been avoided had the applicant sought qualified legal help.

I'm not going to get into the mind-numbing explanations for why many commonly employed tactics — strategies such as placing the name of a child on bank accounts or putting one's home in the name of an heir — are often ineffective or even counterproductive when attempting to qualify for Medicaid assistance.

Let's simply note instead that Medicaid's five-year "look back" at an applicant's assets — an examination that includes a review of how any such assets might have been dispersed during that 60-month window — is a most challenging process. For one thing, regulations regarding the qualification process change frequently, and a plan put in place one year may not be effective two years later. Let's add in passing that people attempting this process on their own have been known to employ tactics that sometimes border on Medicaid fraud.

There are better ways to qualify for Medicaid assistance that might become necessary someday for yourself or a loved one. These ways should involve legally assisted advance planning rather than last-minute shortcuts.

I earlier discussed the concept of asset protection trusts, which allow the orderly transfer of assets into an irrevocable trust that essentially shields such assets from consideration during the five-year look-back review done during the Medicaid qualification process. These trust assets are controlled by your designated trustees who might choose to spend the trust's resources on your care, or they might not. This is a complex trust to establish, however, and requires the assistance of an estate attorney well-versed in the laws of your state.

People pondering the prospect of nursing home confinement without using Medicaid assistance can also prepare by earmarking significant parts of their retirement savings for such a possibility.

Annuities and life insurance policies with living benefit riders are often helpful for this purpose.

Bottom line: The best way to assure your quality of care later in life is through advance planning with qualified assistance rather than trying to beat the system. You will need a good team in place to help you do that, and the time to assemble that team is sooner than later.

CHAPTER 9

Making Decisions
With Your Life Savings

W︎e began this book talking about finding the courage to retire, then looked in detail at some of the steps necessary to do so.

In wrapping things up, let's note the final step in this journey ultimately comes down to being comfortable with the idea that you have amassed over the course of your working career a pool of money that can serve you for the rest of your life, however long that may be.

Equally important is developing the confidence to know that you, with the help of your assembled support team, will be a good steward of the retirement assets you've gathered.

This is often easier said than done.

That's because during our working years we typically look ahead to ways of making additional money. Younger workers anticipate promotions, new higher-paying positions. They also have the energy to work overtime or even take a second job. There is always additional money to be made, they often tell themselves, if only we are willing to work hard enough to earn it.

But things change considerably in retirement when we are now voluntarily unemployed.

Sure, you can always continue to work and produce additional income after reaching "retirement age," and many people do. If you do so because you still love what you do, or because working brings you fulfillment and satisfaction, wonderful. But, if you're working because you have to, because you fear you don't have enough retirement savings to live on — well, you're not really truly retired, are you?

Simply put, one major goal in retirement is to be comfortable enough with your pool of assets that you don't have to work if you don't want to.

You ultimately want to become confident enough to look at what you've amassed from a lifetime of daily labor and know you have the means to sustain you and your family for the rest of your life. You want resources that meet not only anticipated recurring expenses but also provide a "rainy day" cushion for expenditures that are common in retirement. You want assets that allow you and a spouse to splurge on yourselves when you can, even if you occasionally have to crimp when you must. You want the ability to be able to look down the road — to know you can travel to your grandkids' graduation or wedding, or even offer them a gift to help with their first home purchase.

You want to be able to feel good about your financial future even though your retirement assets will be relatively fixed, though hardly set in stone. To be sure, you will still seek growth in these assets — enough growth to replace some or much of what you withdraw for income. But you also know that, barring a big inheritance or a lottery win, your retirement accounts aren't likely going to grow appreciably, and you need to be comfortable with that knowledge.

You also need to put yourself in position to be a good steward of these assets. Your retirement assets, after all, are extremely important to you. They represent your life's savings, the reason you worked five days a week (or more) for 40-some years. These are the resources that must sustain you over a period of time that might be longer than you ever imagined possible.

Coming to terms with this prospect is challenging, and this is why I say it takes a lot of courage to retire. But preparing to live a long time on a relatively fixed pool of retirement savings doesn't have to be a discouraging prospect.

The idea of financially preparing to live a long time becomes a bit less daunting when one has contractually guaranteed income to count on. This is the familiar concept of "mailbox income" that arrives on a regular basis from Social Security, a defined-benefit pension or any income plan you've created for yourself, perhaps through an annuity.

There may be adjustments required along the way. Maybe you'll have to take more in supplemental income for a few months or even years to cover a medical need. Or, perhaps your required minimum distributions generate more income than you need, and you are suddenly wondering what to do with this extra cash. Either way, with an understanding of options available to you in retirement, along with the help of the financial support team you've assembled, such adjustments can be made well into retirement, as I hope to illustrate in the example just below.

Again, the key here is to develop the confidence that you (along with those you've chosen to help you) will be a competent manager of your hard-earned life's savings. The best way to acquire that confidence is through knowledge, some of which I've tried to supply in this book.

You need to know, for instance, how to set reasonable income expectations in retirement based on your asset limitations. This means establishing and following a budget that takes income in a controlled, strategic and methodical manner that measures withdrawals against growth. You need to make informed decisions about when to begin taking Social Security, as well as understand spousal and survivor benefits. You need to prepare for higher medical costs by fully understanding your Medicare and Medigap alternatives. You need to understand your options for financing long-term nursing care. Finally, should legacy giving be important to you, you want to know you have set up an orderly transfer of any assets you wish to pass on to heirs.

Advance planning can help you accomplish all of the above objectives. There will be unexpected events and challenges, no doubt, and planning for these is another essential part of retirement planning. It's when you finally have such a plan in place that you fully develop the confidence to know you can live a long time on your life's savings and thus find the courage to say, "I've had enough of the daily work grind, and I have enough to retire comfortably."

It's never too late to adjust

John and Mary Phillips were well into their 70s — John was 78, Mary a few years younger — when I first met them. They immediately stunned me by announcing that they would like to retire.

To say I was surprised to learn they were still working something close to full time is an understatement. It turns out they owned and worked a farm in addition to managing multiple rental properties that provided them income. Most of their life savings were invested in the rental properties. Managing rental properties is a tough grind — something I learned in doing it myself as a much younger man — and the couple finally decided they'd had enough of collecting rents and making frequent repairs. They wanted to see if they could sell their rental apartments and live off the income for the rest of their lives. Frankly, they seemed a bit daunted by the prospect of making what was to them a dramatic change. They had a ton of questions about disposing of property that had been such a huge part of their lives. How can we be assured of receiving fair market value? they wondered. How do we handle the taxes? Most important, will the money produced by this sale take care of both of us for the rest of our lives?

Clearly, they were not comfortable with the idea of making important decisions with their life savings. When presented such a situation — that is, clients seeking guidance — I generally try to inform them of their options. Although every individual client's situation and resolution will be different, here are a few things we may think about as we work together to address their concerns:

We might talk first about the need to determine the fair market value of their property through a professional real estate appraisal service. We might then encourage our prospective sellers to network with one or more local Realtors to find a buyer willing to pay that fair-market value. That could result in the need to consult with a tax professional to discuss ways to address the tax liability from the sale of the property. If, perhaps, they found a buyer and a sales price is agreed upon, we might talk about finding a reputable title company to assist in closing the sale of the property.

For families like the Phillipses, their goal is to take whatever pool of money they can generate from selling those properties and make that money last for the rest of their lives.

When I have clients like John and Mary, who've saved and invested their whole lives, here are some things we might routinely discuss to help make their nest egg last for the rest of their lives:

One consideration is the tax liability of the property sales — liquidating large assets often comes with a significant tax bill, so we might first set aside money from the sales to cover taxes. We'll then likely talk about how to get lifetime income from the remainder. From my experience, most people entering retirement — particularly those who are John and Mary's age — are interested in protecting at least a portion of their assets from losses, as well as realizing at least some growth in their account.

If our main objective is turning a pool of money into lifelong income, I may suggest we look at an annuity, perhaps a fixed index annuity for at least a part of their portfolio. These remain the only tools I know of to provide protection from loss of principal, as well as provide interest-crediting and contractually guaranteed income for life.

After accounting for the conservative portion of our assets, we would need to talk about taking income from the account when it makes sense for their situation, and possibly with the opportunity to increase that withdrawal rate in time as a retiree's need for income grows due to health concerns or long-term care needs that are a natural part of getting older. As a general rule of thumb, our goal is to attempt to create interest-credited growth that is close to or nearly equal to the rate being withdrawn from income when possible.

Our plan, in short, for couples such as John and Mary would be to take the asset that had supported them for all the years they worked it and turn it into an asset that would support them for the rest of their lives long after they stopped working.

A never-ending goal: To increase an investor's knowledge level

The story of the Phillips family illustrates another point I want to make before ending this book. That is, the importance of seeking professional guidance and help in making and understanding the financial decisions that are most important to you.

I've known clients with strong educational backgrounds and great expertise in their chosen fields who nonetheless struggle to comprehend the many choices available to them in financial matters. This isn't a criticism, but rather a reflection on the often-complex nature of these options.

This complexity is usually a byproduct of the vast array of financial products available from banks, insurance companies or investment firms. These different products are designed to serve different purposes, and some are more appropriate than others at different stages of our lives. Life insurance, for instance, offers death benefit protection to survivors against loss of income should a family's main earner meet an untimely end. Medical insurance protects our assets from devastation in the event of a catastrophic illness. Savings and investment vehicles provide future funds for a college education, the purchase of a first home or eventually retirement among a variety of other purposes.

However, the act of simply purchasing one of these products, while a good start, is never enough.

A consumer also needs a thorough understanding of how each such product will serve his or her individual needs. This understanding should ideally come about before investing in a financial product, especially as it regards the suitability of a product to the individual buying it. This background should include a basic understanding of the product's total cost, its benefits, limitations and restrictions, its risk of loss, its potential for growth, its prospects for future income and the tax implications of that future income.

Here is where the help of a financial advisor, one in whom you believe you can place your trust, is so important.

This person must be more than a good salesperson. Your financial advisor also has to be something of an educator as well as someone who has your best interest in mind. This advisor must be able to fully explain how any financial product will function now and in the future on both a cost and benefit basis. And most importantly, any financial tools he or she might recommend must be in your best interest, not theirs.

The financial services industry in recent years has attempted not only to grow and diversify the kinds of products it makes available, but also to expand the knowledge consumers have about these widely varied products. Information serves as a safeguard that can help keep investors from making bad decisions in a world of ever-expanding financial options.

Providing that kind of information is the main reason I wrote this book. My hope is that the readers who have made it this far will come to better understand the inner workings of some financial tools that can play a big role in a person's financial future in the years leading up to and into retirement. I also hope readers now realize why I favor some financial tools over others, especially when it comes to retirement.

As you've read many times throughout the course of this book, fixed index insurance products headline my list of personal preferences. Tools such as the fixed index annuity or indexed life insurance products offer a combination of both insurance and accumulation possibilities. As I've noted on numerous occasions and will repeat one final time here at the end, they offer what most people nearing or in retirement want most for at least a portion of their portfolio. That is:

Protection against loss of invested principal due to market volatility;

The potential for growth;

A source of regular income that can last for the rest of your life with the properly structured annuity, or work to the benefit of survivors with life insurance as well as some annuities.

These kinds of options are what I mean when I talk about "simple solutions in a complex world."

Though the features and rules of annuities and indexed life insurance can be complex — which is why advisors such as myself are available to explain them — their basic tenets are easily explained.

You are purchasing a product that contractually guarantees it will not lose principal based on market fluctuations, and that guarantee is backed by the claims-paying ability of the issuing insurer. You are purchasing a product that has the potential for conservative growth. With an annuity, you are purchasing a product that will produce a stream of income contractually guaranteed to live on as long as you do. With life insurance, you are purchasing a product that can offer a death benefit that may significantly exceed the premiums paid, assuming the death benefit value isn't depleted by withdrawals from the contract.

Let's go back to something I talked about in the preface to this book. My approach to retirement planning may seem overly simplified to some people, who have reason to believe that few things are ever so simple. But it's equally true that many times in life we make things a whole lot more difficult than they have to be. Retirement is not the time to make things more difficult. I will always believe that financially sound yet simple investment principles such as principal protection and conservative growth can carry the day in retirement, a time where simplification is something worth seeking.

Wrapping it up: Service after the sale

Most people in the financial services industry — be they an insurance agent or an investment broker or a registered investment advisor — sell products. I would suggest that most of these products adequately perform the function for which they are intended, especially when the product addresses the specific needs of the investor. I would further suggest that many agents, brokers and advisors do a reasonably capable job of answering client questions, though some (sadly) do this better before the sale than after it.

Please allow me to close my first book by noting some "service after the sale" aspects of my company, The Resource Center, that I believe are unique from what other companies offer.

The Resource Center has always been more than a place to sell insurance and investment products. Our approach has always been, and will always be, about service to our clients. Sure, all insurance and investment companies say that. Most truly mean it. The difference, I maintain, comes in production as opposed to promise.

"Service after the sale" should be more than just an advertising slogan. At my company, it means doing many different things that all come together in a big picture.

These are things such as the meetings my 14-member staff conducts in anticipation of a severe weather event, during which we plan to make ourselves even more available for the damage claims we might receive in the upcoming days. Things such as offering the services of Skip Wilson, my own staff professional on health insurance and Medicare, Medicaid and Medicare supplements. Things such as our website, www.resourcecenterinc.com, which offers more than basic information about our insurance and investment products, as well as an introduction to our staff. All websites do that. But we also offer helpful articles and videos, among them my regular financial insight segments broadcast on a local TV station.

People such as Skip, myself and some of my other team members at The Resource Center have been in this business for a long time. We're at the point now where our primary goal is to help as many people as we can while we can. This is not an act of philanthropy. We also believe a byproduct of helping people is the chance to grow our business through referrals and word-of-mouth advertising. To me, this seems a natural outgrowth of trying to do the right thing all the time.

Improving client knowledge — helping you make a more informed decision about the financial options that might work best for your specific situation — remains my main goal. It's my reason for writing this book.

I also hope this book is a reflection on my late father. Dad meant so much to me in my years as an insurance salesman, and in the tough decision to begin my own company. His positive outlook was something that will stay with me all my life. "Today was the best day of my life," he would often say. "And tomorrow will be even better."

He also taught me much of what I know today about building personal relationships with clients, with staff, with people in the community who can help as business partners or personal resources.

For readers of this book looking to find the courage to retire, allow me to repeat for a final time that a key to doing this is to build relationships with a network of people who can guide you into and through the years of retirement. The center of this network should be a trusted financial advisor, preferably one with a background in retirement income planning built around the concepts of principal protection, income and the potential for at least conservative growth. This person must be more than a skillful product salesman. You also are looking for an educator, a long-term planner and a navigator who can guide you through the various mazes of Social Security, Medicare, nursing home care and legacy planning.

As my Dad often said, you are looking for someone to help you cross the swollen creek, knowing there is a way to do so.

About the Author

Bruce Porter, a lifelong native of southwestern Missouri, began a career of dealing with the public in his late teens when he first began managing his family's rental properties shortly after his father experienced a heart attack at the too-young age of 38. After attending Missouri State University, in an effort to help support his family's growing real estate business, Porter became licensed to sell real estate and later went into the insurance business.

Even while working to help support his family throughout high school and college, he managed to compete on his high school track and cross country teams, and later continued his athletic career with his college track team as a pole vaulter. He was accepted to train at the prestigious Olympic Training Center in Colorado Springs in 1979. After years of working with a prominent national insurance company during which he became a top salesman and later was promoted to sales management, Porter established his own company, The Resource Center, in 2001 in Springfield.

Designed to be a full-service company that provided home, auto and other types of insurance coverage, as well as financial planning services and wealth management, The Resource Center (www.resourcecenter.com) set out to fulfill Porter's goal of educating clients in an effort to help them make the best decisions for themselves. Over the years since the founding of his company, Bruce has opened a home repair company, "Mr. Fix-it Services of the Ozarks," to help those with smaller home-repair needs. He also was a founding investor in a Springfield community bank, OakStar Bank.

Bruce regularly hosts a weekly TV segment, "Dollars & Sense," on Ozarks Live, a weekly lifestyle program on Springfield station KOLR channel 10.

Bruce and his wife, Deb, are the parents of four children: Kailee King and grandson Samuel Bruce King; Alec Porter; Wendy Featherston; and Dustin Woosley. He is an active member of James River Church in Ozark, Missouri, where he has been a member of the choir as well as serving on Project Partnership and in the Stronger Men's Conference.

Porter also is an ardent supporter of the Missouri State University Bears as well as the Springfield Cardinals, the Double-A minor-league baseball affiliate of the St. Louis Cardinals. He even spent two enjoyable seasons as the team's designated mascot, "Louie." Included in his community involvement is his service as a board member of the Safe at Home project.

Acknowledgments

This book would have not been possible without the extraordinary support of my current staff members at The Resource Center: Michelle Tyler, Wendy Featherston, Kristin Dyer, Connie Dunn, Marc Helfrecht, David Helfrecht, Bill Helfrecht, Josh Grable, John Schaeffer, Skip Wilson, Matt Gardner, Bill Wagner, Grant Brumley, Lee Weilder and Roy King. Integrity beyond measure, honest, loyal and honorable men and women each and every one; I am blessed each and every day.

Thanks also to my family, who have supported me the past three decades with my demanding schedule and time in building my company and career. To my wife Deb and my daughter Kailee and grandson Samuel Bruce King, my son Alec, my daughter Wendy and my son Dustin. To my sons-in-law, Stuart Featherston and Brian King, for loving my daughters and becoming the husbands and fathers I have prayed for since before they were born.

To my mother, June, for loving me beyond measure and always being a positive influence in my daily life and instilling in me the value of hard work, love and commitment.

To my sister, Belinda, and her husband, Brad Belk, for always being there when I needed them from the beginning.

I also want to personally thank my friend and copy editor, Rick Dean, whose patience and encouragement kept the project going. He piloted my thoughts and wisdom on this important information and was a true catalyst in the production of this retirement tool.

And, to the most inspirational man I've ever known: my father, Neil Floyd Porter. Had I not had the honor and privilege of spending my developing years in his presence, I most likely would never have founded The Resource Center, my Springfield, Missouri-based financial services and insurance company. Without him, there would not have been a book for you to read.

In one of my darkest hours early in my career in 1991, late one evening at my office, I opened an envelope my father had mailed to me with the following words of encouragement, and also a poem with great meaning:

Son,

It's Dad. Hold tightly to your faith; our God is a "BIG GOD."

Great insurance and financial service companies exist to serve policyholders and their beneficiaries. The agent and the secretary, the general agent and the file clerk, the president and the janitor — ALL are servants of, and in the final analysis are paid by, the policyowners. The agency serves by keeping an agency force alive and vital for present and future generations. Our personal dedication must be to so guard physical and mental health as to be able to radiate the enthusiasm which comes from being constructively excited. The first of us and the best of us should be dedicated to people and their insurance and financial problems — not to inanimate things.

Pillars are not indestructible. All weather with age and topple in time. However, having been erected with toil and sacrifice, they are not to be circumvented lightly nor casually overthrown. Motivation, Organization, Dedication ... all of these have stood the tests of time. Erect your own pillars and measure your own problems against them; you may find that many will solve themselves when you do so, and more of the best of you will be available to deal creatively with the opportunities in your life.

Love,

Dad

The tree that never had to fight
for sun and sky and air and light,
but stood out in the open plain
and also got its share of rain.
Never became a forest king,
but lived and died a scrubby thing.

The man who never had to toil
to gain and farm his patch of soil,
who never had to win his share
of sun and sky and light of air,
never became a manly man,
but lived and died as he began.

Good timber does not grow with ease,
the stronger wind, the stronger trees,
the further sky, the greater length,
the more the storm, the more the strength.
The sun and cold, by rain and snow,
in trees and men good timber grow.

Where thickest lies the forest growth,
we find the patriarchs of both.
And they hold council with the stars,
whose broken branches show the scars
of many winds and much of strife;
This is the common law of life.

                    -Douglas Malloch

Made in the USA
Columbia, SC
20 December 2018